JONATHAN SWIFT

JONATHAN SWIFT

by

A. NORMAN JEFFARES

Edited by Ian Scott-Kilvert

PUBLISHED FOR
THE BRITISH COUNCIL
BY LONGMAN GROUP LTD

LONGMAN GROUP LTD
Longman House, Burnt Mill, Harlow, Essex

*Associated companies, branches and
representatives throughout the world*

First published 1976
© A. Norman Jeffares 1976

*Printed in England by
Bradleys, Reading and London*

ISBN 0 582 01248 1

CONTENTS

I. LIFE

JONATHAN SWIFT was born in Dublin on 30 November 1667. His father was the youngest of the five sons of Thomas Swift, vicar of Goodrich and rector of Bridstow in Herefordshire, an ardent royalist who had been ejected from his two livings and imprisoned by the Cromwellians. After his death, the Swifts, attracted by the possibilities of making themselves lucrative careers, came to Ireland. Swift's father, however, died in the March or April before his son's birth, and the widow had merely twenty pounds a year on which to live. Swift described his parents' marriage as 'on both sides very indiscreet, for his wife brought her husband little or no fortune, and his death happening so suddenly before he could make a sufficient establishment for his family.' He remarked that he felt the consequences of that marriage not only through the whole course of his education, but during the greatest part of his life. He did not have a home in the ordinary sense of the word, and when he was about a year old his wet-nurse took him from Dublin to Whitehaven (of which place she was a native), where he stayed for nearly three years. Swift thought he had been, in effect, kidnapped by the nurse because she 'was extremely fond of the infant', and his mother sent orders he was not to hazard another sea voyage back to Dublin until he 'could be better able to bear it'.

After he returned to Ireland he did not stay long with his mother. She returned to England with her daughter, to her home in Leicestershire, and Swift was then brought up by his uncles in Ireland. He was sent, probably at the age of six (in 1673 or 1674), to Kilkenny College, an excellent school established by the Ormond family. He entered Trinity College, Dublin on 24 April 1682. His tutor was St George Ashe, who later became Provost and subsequently held several Bishoprics. Swift's own account of his undergraduate days gives a gloomy picture:

... by the ill treatment of his nearest relations, he was so discouraged and sunk in his spirits, that he too much neglected some parts of his academic studyes, for which he had no great relish by nature, and turned himself to reading history and poetry. So that

5

when the time came for taking his degree of batchelor, although he had lived with great regularity and due observance of the statutes, he was stopped of his degree for dullness and insufficiency, and at last admitted in a manner little to his credit, which is called in that college *speciali gratia*.

Swift had found being a poor relation humiliating. When he was very young he had wanted to be famous. His unhappiness is poignantly recorded in a memory of one youthful moment of frustration, itself an example of other events and emotions:

I remember when I was a little boy, I felt a great fish at the end of my line which I drew up almost on the ground, but it dropt in, and the disappointment vexeth me to this very day, and I believe it was the type of all my future disappointments.

In fact he had the best education to be got in Ireland, and he had not done so badly in Trinity as he made out in his old age. He found the curriculum dull; the most likely career which it led to, the Anglican Church of Ireland, did not necessarily offer the prospect of rapid advancement: and he was short of money. He spent nearly seven years at Trinity College and was about to take his master's degree when public events intervened.

The tensions of impending revolution no doubt explain some of Swift's unsettled state as a student. Admonished for neglect of duties and for 'frequenting the town' in March 1687, he started tumults in College and with five others insulted the Junior Dean in November of that year, for which their degrees were suspended and they had to beg the Junior Dean's pardon publicly on bended knees. James II's appointment of Tyrconnel as Lord Lieutenant led to a withdrawal of the College's annual grant when the authorities refused to appoint a Roman Catholic to a Fellowship on the King's orders. Most of the Fellows and students, Swift among them, joined the general exodus of Protestants to England and Scotland.

After staying some time with his mother in Leicester, Swift became private secretary to Sir William Temple in 1689. Temple had family connexions with Ireland. His grandfather had been Provost of Trinity College, Dublin; his father, Sir

6

John Temple, was educated there, became Master of the Rolls in Ireland but eventually lived in London; Temple himself was elected to the Irish convention of 1660 and became a member of the Dublin parliament in 1661. He pursued a diplomatic career, and was the architect of the triple alliance between England, Sweden and the United Provinces; he next served as ambassador to Holland where he became a close friend of William of Orange. Finally, in dislike of public life, he retreated to the country in 1681. Temple's effect on Swift was profound, for his experience of court life and diplomacy and the elegant mode of life he created at Moor Park, his country place in Surrey, enlarged the young man's horizons and, no doubt, his ambitions. After Swift had experienced his first attack of what we now know as Ménière's disease, (its aetiology was not fully recognized until 1861; its symptoms are giddiness, vomiting, deafness and noises in the head) he returned briefly to Ireland. He thought his giddiness had been caused by eating too many apples (his later deafness he put down to the effects of a severe cold), and the doctors thought the effects of the English climate might have caused his illness. But he was soon back. Life at Moor Park, in a dependent position, however, was not enough for him. Not unnaturally he wanted to make his own way in the world and Temple was 'less forward' than Swift hoped in aiding him to obtain a position in the church. But he had 'a scruple of entering the church meerly for support' so, once he had managed to get Temple to offer him a minor clerkship in the office of the Master of the Rolls in Ireland, he felt he could enter the church from choice rather than necessity. He refused the clerkship and left Moor Park in May 1694. Sir William Temple was 'extremely angry' and still would not promise the young man anything firmly.

Swift returned to Ireland, not realizing that he would have difficulty in becoming ordained. There was a need to explain why he had not entered the church at once after taking his degree. What had he been doing in England? He had to humble himself, to write to Temple for a testimonial testifying to his good life and behaviour, and giving the reasons for his leaving Temple's household. (Temple's sister Lady Giffard endorsed the ensuing dignified appeal to

Temple as Swift's 'penitential' letter). Temple wrote in support of his former secretary; and Swift was ordained as Deacon in October 1694, as priest in January 1695. Two weeks later he became prebend of Kilroot. He found this experience of living in a rural parish in Northern Ireland with but a few parishioners, and surrounded by Presbyterians, disheartening, and he gave up the living at Temple's persuasion and returned to Moor Park in 1696.

In 1699, however, Temple died without having obtained a living for Swift in England as he had promised he would, and so Swift again travelled to Ireland, this time as chaplain to the Earl of Berkeley (who had become one of the three Lords Justice). The following year he was appointed vicar of Laracor in Co. Meath and became a prebend of St Patrick's Cathedral in Dublin. Again he was in a parish very thinly peopled with Church of Ireland Protestants, but this time he was surrounded by Catholics. He liked the place, and set about gardening, planting and improving his grounds.

When he was at Kilroot he had courted Jane Waring of Belfast, whom he knew as Varina. It was a curious courtship. He wrote her eloquent letters but she did not fancy living in Kilroot on Swift's income. He managed to extricate himself by asking her to commit herself immediately when he was going back to Moor Park in 1696, though he was obviously fairly confident she would not do so. He had realistic views about marriage. He had earlier been involved in heavy flirtations in Leicester, but he regarded himself as naturally temperate and he said there were always 'a thousand household thoughts' to drive matrimony out of his mind whenever it chanced to come there. In 1699 he wrote a series of seventeen resolutions entitled 'When I come to be old', the first, fifth and fifteenth of which are part of what John Forster called in his biography 'the mystery' of Swift's life: they are 'Not to marry a young woman'; 'Not to be fond of children, or let them come near me hardly'; 'Not to hearken to flatteries, nor conceive I can be beloved by a young woman; *et eos qui haereditatem captant, odisse ac vitare*.[1]' When he was once more in Ireland, in Laracor, Varina wrote to enquire why he had not visited her in Belfast, and, in effect, he

[1] Translation: 'and to hate and avoid those who practise legacy-hunting'.

8

dismissed her, in 1700, in a devastating letter full of challenging questions: as to whether she had good enough health, ability to manage a household on perhaps less than £300 a year, and an adequate inclination to his person and humours for marriage with him. There was another reason for ending their relationship. He had first met Esther Johnson, whom he later called Stella, at Moor Park when she was a child of thirteen (some critics have agreed that Sir William Temple may have been her father); he now persuaded her to move to Ireland in 1701 with a friend and companion, Rebecca Dingley. He had taught Stella at Moor Park; she was intelligent, truthful and courageous: she fitted into his idea of friendship. He never saw her alone, though the two ladies lived at Laracor and in his Dublin residences when he was not there. It was an unusual relationship. Swift wrote in 1704 to William Tisdall, a clergyman and friend of his who wished to marry Stella, that if his own fortunes and humour 'served me to think of that state, I should certainly among all persons on earth, make your choice; because I never saw that person whose conversation I entirely valued but hers; this was the utmost I ever gave way to'. When he wrote to her he addressed his letters to both ladies, and his close and tender friendship with Stella lasted, with perhaps one break, till her death in 1728.

Swift was in London with Berkeley in 1701, and he then wrote his first political pamphlet, *A Discourse of the Contests and Dissentions between the Nobles and the Commons in Athens and Rome*. This praised the Whig leaders Somers and Halifax (disguised under Roman names), and the following year Swift let himself be known in London as the author. He made several visits to England between April 1701 and 1704. In 1704 came the anonymous publication of *A Tale of a Tub* and *The Battle of the Books* (even in the fifth edition the anonymity was kept up), though the identity of the author was known to Swift's peers. Swift intended *A Tale of A Tub* as a satire on what he thought the gross contemporary corruptions in religion and learning: in it he satirized the worldliness of Rome and the immoderacy of the Presbyterians and Nonconformists. He was himself a churchman of the centre, though he called himself a 'high churchman'.

Although he thought the Church of England far from perfect, it was the best church he knew; its doctrine and discipline were moderate and cautious. It offered the middle way between Rome and puritanism. He valued the Anglican church as the voice of reason, and reason seemed very necessary in an age when the Stuarts and the Puritans had recently tried to seize power: both royalist and puritan causes were regarded as leading to absolutism and tyranny. Swift, however, knew man's management of Christianity was all too human; and he was not above exercising his wit on religious absurdity, while remaining a good churchman.

During the period from 1707 to 1709 Swift was in London endeavouring to persuade the Whig government to grant a concession, remission of the first-fruits[1] and tithes, to the Church of Ireland. His efforts were unsuccessful and he was also disappointed in his attempts to gain preferment. It was hinted to him that the remission of the first-fruits might be granted if the Test Act were to be repealed in Ireland. The Whigs' policy was to repeal the sacramental Test, and by removing it in Ireland they might have a useful example to support their removal of this measure in England also. It was an Act which excluded non-Anglicans from political power. Through its operation the Dissenters and Catholics could not, for instance, accept commissions in the army and the militia. Swift, however, was deeply concerned about the position of the Anglican church. He believed there was a danger of upsetting what had been achieved; he disliked the potential for corruption which might be generated by change; equilibrium was a condition for the continuance of the Anglican church and balanced government. But in Ireland the numbers of Protestant churchmen in the Pale[2] was small, the Establishment was insecure, and Swift felt the Dissenters of Scottish descent in the north had an innate industry and bravery as well as 'a most formidable notion of episcop[ac]y', which they thought, 'as most surely they did', three degrees worse than popery. It is clear that *A Letter from a*

[1] The first year's income or profits, formerly paid by each new holder of a benefice, or any office of profit, to some superior (S.O.E.D.).

[2] The Pale: that part of Ireland over which English jurisdiction was established (S.O.E.D.).

Member of the House of Commons in Ireland to a Member of the House of Commons in England concerning the Sacramental Test (which Swift dated as from Dublin in December 1708) that his distrust of the Presbyterians was far greater than any worry about the Catholics, who had, after all, been defeated:

'Tis agreed among naturalists that a lion is a larger, a stronger, and more dangerous enemy than a cat; yet if a man were to have his choice, either a lion at his foot, bound fast with three or four chains, his teeth drawn out, and his claws pared to the quick, or an angry cat in full liberty at his throat; he would take no long time to determine.

It was probably in the summer of 1708 that Swift's friendship with Addison ripened into close intimacy: it was then that he complained of increased governmental work preventing Addison from meeting him as often as he would wish: their respect and liking for each other was mutual. Addison inscribed a copy of his *Travels in Italy* to 'the most Agreeable Companion, the Truest friend and the Greatest Genius of his Age'; and Swift regarded Addison as the man who had 'worth enough to give reputation to our age'. A remark is attributed to Swift that when he and Addison spent an evening together they 'neither of them ever wished for a third person': they were, however, often in the company of wits (largely Whigs) and Swift also formed a friendship with Addison's friend and schoolfellow Richard Steele. He aided Steele in the creation of *The Tatler* and wrote pieces for it. Ambrose Philips and Matthew Prior were other friends of this period and he had met many other literary figures in the coffee-house society of the time, in which his school fellow Congreve, a member of the Whigs' Kit Kat Club, also moved freely. Yet another friend was Charles Ford, a smart young intellectual and Irish landowner.

In the summer of 1709 Swift returned to Ireland in a depressed state. The symptoms of Ménière's disease, the giddiness, nausea, deafness and noises in his head, continued throughout his life, and there are many entries in his memoranda book which show his occasional utter despair, two poignant examples being the entries for April 1709—'Small giddy fitt and swimming in the head MD (his name for

Stella) and God help me'—and July 1710—'Terrible fitt.
God knows what may be the event. Better towards the end.'
Despite these attacks he enjoyed his time at Laracor, planting
trees, improving his garden, mending his canal. He had much
social life. Addison was secretary to the Lord Lieutenant and
Swift saw a good deal of him in Dublin, introducing him to
Stella—they liked each other—and there were many other
friends with whom to dine and play cards.

When, somewhat reluctantly ('I never went to England
with so little desire in my life'), he returned to London in
1710, things began to change. Though the letters to Stella and
Miss Dingley in Dublin continued with all their openness,
their constant account of his doings and ideas, they did not
convey the complication of a new friendship he began or
perhaps drifted into with Esther Vanhomrigh. His relationship with Esther—he called her Hessy or Vanessa—(he was
forty-one, she twenty) was based on a teasing, didactic,
almost fatherly concern for her intellectual and moral
development: and she (whose father was dead) found it
irresistible. He dined frequently at the Vanhomrighs in the
autumn and winter of 1710; in the spring Mrs Vanhomrigh
set aside a room for him. Stella was surprised at his frequenting
them; he replied in a letter, jocosely but perhaps also de-
fensively, 'You say they are of no consequence: why, they
keep as good female company as I do male; I see all the drabs
of quality at this end of town with them . . .'. On the one hand
he taught Vanessa to despise orthodox views of conventional
behaviour; on the other he valued discretion; he was probably quite sure of his own propriety, he had no intention of
marrying, but he did enjoy his intimate friendship with this
attractive girl. It is possible that she declared her love for
him in 1712; it was probably in the autumn of 1713 that he
wrote the poem Cadenus and Vanessa which gives us an idea
of his evasive tactics when Vanessa indicated her preference
for passion rather than a platonic friendship:

> But friendship in its greatest height
> A constant, rational delight
> On virtue's basis fix'd to last,
> When love's allurements long are past;
> Which gently warms but cannot burn;

He gladly offers in return:
His want of passion will redeem,
With gratitude, respect, esteem:
With that devotion we bestow
When goddesses appear below.

Conversations with Vanessa, those meetings 'over a pott of coffee or an orange and sugar in the sluttery, which I have so often found to be the most agreeable chamber in the world', provided a relief from the world of politics, where Swift was rapidly becoming so successful. The new Tory Ministry realized the value of his combination of cold reason and explosive logic, and agreed to remission of the first-fruits (though Swift did not get the credit for this). He became a close friend of Harley and St John, and was put in charge of the Tory journal *The Examiner*. This was the beginning of his period of political power.

After the Tory administration came into office, Swift had used his influence on behalf of Whig writers, as he told Stella in a letter:

And do you know I have taken more pains to recommend the Whig wits to the favour and mercy of the ministers than any other people. Steele I have kept in his place; Congreve I have got to be used kindly, and secured. Rowe I have recommended and got a promise of a place. Philips I could certainly have provided for, if he had not run party mad and made me withdraw my recommendation; and I got Addison so right at first, that he might have been employed, and have partly secured him the place he has; yet I am worse used by that faction than any man.

He tried to reconcile Steele and Harley, but Steele did not keep the appointment. Later in 1713 he quarrelled fiercely with Swift. Relations with Addison were not easy because of party differences, and John Arbuthnot, the Queen's physician, became Swift's closest companion and friend. He shared Swift's love of hoaxes, of paradox, of irony. Swift had met him at Windsor. His friendship with the ministers had led him to court, where he had a wide range of acquaintances. He dined with the great, indeed he was included in 'The Society', a dining club set up by St John for men of 'wit and interest', whose members called each other Brother. Another grouping, the Scriblerus Club, was made up of leading writers, Swift, Arbuthnot, Pope, Gay and Parnell, who allowed Harley and St John to attend their meetings. A love of satiric literature and erudite jesting was shared by these authors, and their meetings obviously gave Swift very great pleasure. It was an exciting period in his life, and portions of 'The Author upon Himself' convey this:

> Swift had the sin of wit, no venial crime;
> Nay 'twas affirm'd he sometimes dealt in rhyme
> Humour and mirth had place in all he writ;
> He reconcil'd divinity and wit:
> He moved and bow'd, and talk'd with too much grace;
> Nor show'd the parson in his gait or face;
> Despis'd luxurious wines and costly meat;
> Yet still was at the tables of the great;
> Frequented lords; saw those that saw the queen,
> At Child's or Truby's never once had been.

Though he did not bother to frequent the favourite taverns of the clergy, Child's and Truby's, he worked hard for his view of how the interests of church and state should be preserved. His skill as a political propagandist greatly aided the acceptance of Tory policies and, notably, his attacks on Marlborough, which helped to bring about the conclusion of the war against France. *The Conduct of the Allies*, which went through many editions, supplied the arguments for the debate in the House of Commons: as he told Stella 'The Resolutions printed t'other day in the Votes are almost quotations from it; and would never have passed, if that book had not been written'. His pen, however, had harmed his own career as well as Marlborough's, for *A Tale of a Tub* had been described to Queen Anne as profane. The 'royal prude', as Swift called her, was reluctant that he should occupy high office in the Church. He had used this phrase in a lampoon upon the Duchess of Somerset, the mistress of the robes, who henceforth became his implacable enemy. This was partly because Swift had published the third part of Sir William Temple's *Memoirs* against the wishes of the family; these reflected upon the character of Lord Essex, husband of the Duchess's favourite aunt. So he was not given the fat English deanery or slim bishopric he desired, but instead was made Dean of St Patrick's Cathedral, Dublin, in April 1713. This post Swift regarded as a kind of exile, deeply regretting the distance from his friends in London. He was soon back in London, trying to patch up affairs between the two estranged Tory leaders, then withdrawing to the country, hoping to be made Historiographer Royal, finally deciding to withdraw with Harley, now Earl of Oxford, after Bolingbroke had won and Oxford had been dismissed. Then the Queen died, and the Whigs were back in power with the Hanoverian King enthroned.

In Ireland Swift occupied himself with administration. 'You are to understand', he wrote to Pope

That I live in the corner of a vast unfurnished house. My family consists of a steward, a groom, a helper in the stable, a footman, and an old maid, who are all at board wages, and when I do not dine abroad, or make an entertainment, which last is very rare, I eat a mutton-pie, and drink half a pint of wine. My amusements are defending my small dominions against the Archbishop, and endeavouring to reduce my rebellious choir.

He worked on *Gulliver's Travels*, and after about three years had found congenial company, two clergymen, younger wits and scholars, Thomas Sheridan and Patrick Delany. It was not, however, as brilliant a society as he had left in London he wrote to Pope in 1722:

The best and greatest part of my life, until these eight years, I spent in England, there I made my friendships, and there I left my desires. I am condemned for ever to another country; what is in prudence to be done?

A crisis arose in his relationship with Vanessa, who had crossed to Ireland in 1714 despite the stern warning he had given her in England, 'If you are in Ireland while I am there, I shall see you very seldom. It is not a place for any freedom, but where everything is known in a week, and magnified a hundred degrees.' She seemed earlier to have accepted his conditions for friendship; but despite his warnings she was importunate; he reminded her again that he would see her seldom. There was some final break, perhaps because she realized that the friendship for Stella came first with him. In June he vanished to the south of Ireland for several months. Vanessa had died, on the last day of May 1723, making no mention of him in her will. He was in the depths of depression when he wrote to Pope in September.

I read the most trifling books I can find, and whenever I write, it is upon the most trifling subjects; but riding, waking, and sleeping take up eighteen of the twenty-four hours. I procrastinate more than I did twenty years ago, and have several things to finish which I put off to twenty years hence.

Irish politics, however, roused him from his inertia, the Drapier[1] was born, and *Gulliver's Travels* finished. He wrote a famous letter to Pope about them on 29 September 1725 which contained his rationale as man and writer:

I have ever hated all nations, professions and communities, and all my love is towards individuals: for instance, I hate the tribe of lawyers, but I love Counsellor Such-a-one, and Judge Such-a-one . . . But principally I hate and detest that animal called man, although I heartily love John, Peter, Thomas, and so forth.

He arrived in London in 1726, took up his old friendships after twelve years, and argued Ireland's case unsuccessfully with Walpole.

He was deeply disturbed at news of Stella's illness when in London and wrote some letters, to his sub-dean Worrall, to Stopford and to Sheridan, which show how affected he was. 'We have been perfect friends these thirty-five years,' he wrote, explaining how he had realized how ill she was, and how much her death would mean to him. 'I am of the opinion that there is not a greater folly than to contract too great and intimate a friendship, which must always leave the survivor miserable.' He tried to rationalize the situation, but Stella 'excelled in every good quality', and he confessed that 'violent friendship is much more lasting, and as much engaging, as violent love'. She recovered, but the ordeal of her death was deferred only for a year. In that year he offered her a last birthday poem:

1 See page 32.

From not the greatest of divines
Accept for once some serious lines

In this he allowed his affection to have its head. He was again in London—his last visit to England—in 1727 and was himself ill when the news of her being again in a precarious state reached him in September. Ill as he was, he rushed off to Holyhead as soon as he could, only to find himself, with wind and tide unfavourable for a week, raging at the delay. Stella died in January and he immediately wrote an account of her life, finding it impossible to attend the burial service, the lights of which he saw through the Deanery window as he recorded Stella's qualities. This brief biography is haunting in its simplicity and sorrow.

Swift's last years were filled with more activity on behalf of Ireland. To this period belongs *A Modest Proposal* (1729) and *Verses on the Death of Dr Swift* (1731), virtually a posthumous survey of his own life. He was also involved in *A Complete Collection of Genteel and Ingenious Conversations* and the *Directions to Servants*. He was often ill now, irascible at times, and yet his fierce anger flared out as effectively as ever in 'The Legion Club', his scathing attack on the Dublin parliament. His popularity, he wrote to Pope, was 'wholly confined to the common people who are more constant than those we miscall our betters'. When he walked the streets, he was received with acclaim, his seventieth birthday celebrated with illuminations, bonfires and salutes of guns. And yet his attitude to the 'ordinary' people of Ireland was ambivalent, indeed paradoxical; while condemning their governors, he despised them for their inability to help themselves. As his friend Arbuthnot recorded, he was a sincere, honest man who spoke truth when others were afraid to speak it. He himself wrote of his hate

Whose lash just Heaven had long decreed
Shall on a day make sin and folly bleed.

At the age of fifty he had said to Edward Young, when gazing at the elm tree withered and decayed in its upper branches, 'I shall be like that tree: I shall die at the top'. His memory went; a letter, written in 1740 to his cousin Mrs

Whiteway, described his miserable state: extremely deaf and full of pain. He was 'so stupid and confounded' he could not express the mortification he was under in body and mind. He was sure his days would be few. Alas, he lived another five years, found by a Commission in 1742 not to be capable of taking care of his person or fortune. He died on 19 October 1745, and was buried in the Cathedral, with the Latin epitaph he wrote for himself placed over his grave. Yeats's version of it gives us the essence of the man:

> Swift has sailed into his rest;
> Savage indignation there
> Cannot lacerate his breast.
> Imitate him if you dare,
> World-besotted traveller; he
> Served human liberty.

II. THE PROSE SATIRES

A Tale of a Tub
Swift finished 'the greatest part' of *A Tale of a Tub* in 1696 and published it anonymously in 1704. It was wrapped around in the mystery with which Swift loved to tease his readers; he seems to have assumed a false identity—a *persona*. In the fourth document, fitted in between 'The Dedication to Lord Somers' and 'The Epistle Dedicatory . . . to Prince Posterity', and entitled 'The Bookseller to the Reader' it is stated that no satisfaction can be given as to the author, the bookseller being credibly informed that the publication is 'without his knowledge' and whether the author had finished it or intended to fill up the defective places 'is like to remain a secret'. This challenging the curiosity of readers about the identity of the supposed author was matched by the mass of learned allusions in which the book abounds. The supposed annotator says 'I believe one of the Author's Designs was to set curious Men a-hunting thro Indexes and enquiring for Books out of the Common Road'. He issued a warning to those 'whom the *Learned* among Posterity will appoint for Commentators upon this elaborate Treatise' and, as Professor

Nichol Smith, himself one of Swift's most notable modern editors, remarked, 'the modern editor must always be conscious of the shade of Swift finding amused pleasure in the false surmises that send him searching on the wrong track, and when the hunt is successful, as often by luck as by skill, in the explanations that sometimes come perilously near to pedantry'.

Swift's reading was extremely wide and in his own words 'indefatigable'; he kept commonplace books, he abstracted from authors, he epitomized, but ultimately he was his own man, sceptical yet creative, insisting proudly that he had not borrowed hints from any other writers in the world. His originality is born out by his own style, highly individual even in the midst of its mocking parodies. In *A Tale of a Tub* Swift involved himself in satirizing abuses in religion with digressions which mocked abuses in learning, literature and language. He wrote in the manner of earlier seventeenth-century prose writers, echoing their complexity, and the magnificent manner of their rhetoric. The following passage on man's fancy is characteristic: it is metaphysical in its imaginative energy, its paradoxical exaggeration, and contradictory in that it condemns the very fancy or free imagination which gives it exuberant life:

AND, whereas the mind of Man, when he gives the Spur and Bridle to his Thoughts, doth never stop, but naturally sallies out into both extremes of High and Low, of Good and Evil; his first flight of fancy, commonly transports Him to Idea's of what is most Perfect, finished, and exalted; till having soared out of his own Reach and Sight, not well perceiving how near the Frontiers of Height and Depth, border upon each other; With the same Course and Wing, he falls down plum into the lowest Bottom of Things; like one who travels the *East* into the *West*; or like a strait line drawn by its own length into a Circle. Whether a Tincture of Malice in our Natures, makes us fond of furnishing every bright Idea with its Reverse; Or, whether Reason reflecting upon the Sum of Things, can, like the Sun, serve only to enlighten one half of the Globe, leaving the other half, by Necessity, under the Shade and Darkness; Or, whether Fancy, flying up to the imagination of what is Highest and Best, becomes over-shot, and spent, and weary, and suddenly falls like a dead Bird of Paradise, to the Ground.

He could draw upon earlier writers. For instance, this passage from *Antony and Cleopatra* (IV, 14):

> Sometimes we see a cloud thats dragonish;
> A vapour sometime like a bear or a lion,
> A tower'd citadel, a pendant rock,
> A forked mountain, or blue promontory
> With trees upon't, that nod unto the world
> And mock our eyes with air

was pressed into his service

> If I should venture in a windy Day, to affirm to *Your Highness*, that there is a large Cloud near the *Horizon* in the Form of a *Bear*, another in the *Zenith* with the Head of an *Ass*, a third to the Westward with Claws like a *Dragon*; and *Your Highness* should in a few Minutes think fit to examine the Truth, 'tis certain, they would all be changed in Figure and Position, new ones would arise, and all we could agree upon would be, that Clouds there were, but that I was grossly mistaken in the *Zoography* and *Topography* of them.

Swift was a firm believer in common sense; he wrote as a wit and a literary man. He naturally deflated what he thought dangerous and stupid. Thus he moved to a simpler style when he recounted the actual *Tale*. This is the allegorical story— it begins 'Once upon a time'—of the man 'who had Three Sons by one Wife, and all at a Birth, neither could the Mid-Wife tell certainly which was the Eldest.' The Father leaves his triplet sons each a coat instructing them not to alter them in any way. These coats represent the Christian faith, the sons Peter, Martin and Jack the three churches: Peter the Roman Catholic, Martin the Lutheran which becomes the Anglican after the Reformation, and Jack the Calvinist. Peter departs from the terms of the will after ingenious interpretations of it, so that silver fringes, embroidery and shoulder knots are added. He hides the will and goes mad. The others, ejected from his house, get copies of the will and realize how they have departed from its conditions. Martin takes away as much as he can of the added decoration without damaging the original cloth, but Jack damages his coat by tearing off the extra material, being more bent on removing Peter's influence than keeping to the will. Peter's belief in the infallibility of the Pope and Jack's in his own interpretation of the Bible lead to corruption in religion, but Martin, who represents the Anglicanism in which Swift believed, was rational in his attitude to religion—the compromise achieved was between Christianity and the world, and based upon the actual historical situation. The dangers to the Anglican position from Catholicism and Dissent were added to by the effects of the Deists, notably John Locke, the author of the *Essay Concerning Human Understanding* and the *Sceptics*, notably Thomas Hobbes, author of *Leviathan*. Swift attacked both viewpoints in *A Tale of a Tub*, particularly in the Digression on Madness. Ironically he praises man's capacity for self delusion:

... when a Man's Fancy gets *Astride* on his Reason, when Imagination is at Cuffs with the Senses and Common Understanding, as well as Common Sense, is Kickt out of Doors; the first Proselyte he makes, is Himself, and when that is once compass'd, the Difficulty is not so great in bringing over others; A Strong Delusion always operating from *without*, as vigorously as from *within*. For, Cant and Vision are to the Ear and Eye, the same as Tickling is to the Touch. Those Entertainments and Pleasures we most value in life, are such a *Dupe* and play the Wag with the Senses.

Swift had developed his own style: he depended in part upon lulling his reader into false security and then exposing the falsity of his reasoning, his happiness which '*is a perpetual Possession of being well Deceived*'. There is a passage which praises the pursuit of truth despite the pain this may cause:

And therefore, in order to save the Charges of all such expensive Anatomy for the time to come; I do here think fit to inform the Reader that in such Conclusions as these, Reason is certainly in the Right; and that in most Corporeal Beings which have fallen under my Cognizance, the *Outside* hath been infinitely preferable to the *In*: Whereof I have been farther convinced from some late Experiments. Last week I saw a Woman *flay'd* and you will hardly believe how much it altered her Person for the worse.

Despite the anonymity of its authorship, *A Tale of a Tub*, reprinted twice in 1704 and again in 1705, made Swift's reputation, but it marred his career in the church, for, although we can now see its essential morality, it offended many by what Atterbury called its 'profane strokes'. Swift defended it in the Apology which prefaced the fifth edition of 1710; but he had not perhaps fully realized how few people could—and still can—accept a relationship between satire and genuine religion such as that which he put forward with what Nigel Dennis has described as 'so much coarseness and vehemence'. He had to create an audience for his particular invention, the *persona*, the 'author'; his apparent irreverence, his variety of viewpoint, and his shatteringly satiric comments on stupidity have meant that the audience has sometimes shared Queen Anne's unamused disapproval. And Swift knew it. He wrote in 'The Life and Character of Dean Swift' in 1731:

'Tis own'd he was a *Man of Wit-*,
Yet many a *foolish thing* he writ-;
And, sure he must be deeply learn'd-!
That's more than ever I discern'd-;
I know his nearest friends complain
He was too *airy* for a *Dean*.

The Battle of the Books
Along with *A Tale of a Tub* was published *The Battle of the Books*, which reflects some of Swift's unease at the corruptions which he thought had invaded English life and letters after the Civil War: he was particularly concerned about the corruption of the language. He had also a certain scepticism about the value of the new sciences. His defence of Sir William Temple's essay *Of Ancient and Modern Learning* (1690) involved him in an argument in which Temple had cited *Aesop's Fables* and the *Epistles of Phalaris* to prove the superiority of the ancients in prose. William Wotton defended the modern age in his *Reflections upon Ancient and Modern Learning* (1694) and Richard Bentley in the second edition of this book argued that neither the *Fables* nor the *Epistles* were as old as Temple thought. Boyle supported Temple, and Swift joined in the fray—but was strongly aware of what *was* important: he used the mock-heroic form to allow sufficient distance from the actual controversy. Into

his account of the battle in St James's Library (Bentley had been keeper there) he introduced a digression, the fable of the spider and the bee, based upon a proverb, frequently used in the seventeenth century: 'where the bee sucks honey, the spider sucks poison'. Temple had used the image of the bee in his essay *Of Poetry* (1690), and Swift, after dismissing the spider as a symbol of modernity, produced an echo of Temple's poem in praise of the bee, ending with an elegant phrase itself echoed a century and a half later by Matthew Arnold:

... As for *Us*, the *Ancients*, We are content with the *Bee*, to pretend to Nothing of our own beyond our *Wings* and our *Voice*: this is to say, our *Flights* and our *Language*; For the rest, whatever we have got, has been infinite Labor, and search, and ranging thro' every corner of Nature: The Difference is, that instead of *Dirt* and *Poison*, we have rather chose to fill our Hives with *Honey* and *Wax*, thus furnishing Mankind with the two Noblest of Things, which are *Sweetness* and *Light*.

The spider represents the overweening, self-sufficient pride of an age concerned with artifice, rejecting the wisdom of the past, relying on intellect to create new ways of thought. Swift looked back to 'the peaceable part' of the reign of Charles I as the highest period of politeness in England, and when he measured by that standard the world of his own time he found it sadly lacking:

Whether is the nobler Being of the two, That which by a lazy Contemplation of Four Inches round; by an over-weening Pride which feeding and engendering on itself, turns all into Excrement and Venom; producing nothing at last, but Fly-bone and a Cobweb: Or That, which, by an universal Range, with long Search, much Study, true Judgement, and Distinction of Things, brings home Honey and Wax.

Gulliver's Travels

Swift wrote most of *Gulliver's Travels* between 1721 and 1725, not, as used to be thought, between 1714–20 (a theory which led to the idea that Swift wrote the book on his return to Ireland in disappointment, and that the fourth book was the culmination of his misanthropy. The fourth book, in fact, was written before the third). Some parts may possibly derive from earlier drafts associated with a project of the Scriblerus Club to produce the *Memoirs of Martin Scriblerus* (1741), the satiric remembrances of an invented traveller.

The first edition, printed in London by Benjamin Motte, appeared in 1726; two editions followed in 1727, though Swift was dissatisfied with the text and himself later corrected the version published in 1735 by the Dublin printer George Faulkner (Vol. III of a four-volume edition of Swift's *Works*). Swift's friend Gay wrote to him describing it as 'the conversation of the whole town' since its publication, with all agreed 'in liking it extremely'. And he alluded to the fiction that Swift had nothing to do with it:

'Tis generally said that you are the author, but I am told, the Bookseller declares he knows not from what hand it came. From the highest to the lowest it is universally read, from the Cabinet-council to the Nursery.

Swift himself enjoyed the situation. In a letter to Mrs Howard he remarked that he could not understand a letter of hers 'till a bookseller sent me the Travells of one Captain Gulliver, who proved a very good Explainer, although at the same time, I thought it hard to be forced to read a Book of seven hundred Pages in order to understand a Letter of fifty lines'.

Gulliver's Travels begins with two prefatory items, 'A letter from Captain Gulliver to his Cousin Sympson' and 'The Publisher to the Reader'. These are designed to give authenticity to the accounts of Gulliver's four voyages which follow. Swift was writing in well-established genres, the traveller's tale, and parodies of it. He drew upon a very entertaining parody of fabulous voyages (such as those we find in the *Odyssey* and elsewhere in classical literature)— probably the first of its kind—written by Lucian in the second century AD. The hero of Lucian's *True History* had many adventures, including being blown up to the moon and living for two years inside a whale. Sir Thomas More's Introduction to *Utopia* (1516), the fourth and fifth books of Rabelais (c. 1547) and Cyrano de Bergerac's *Histoire Comique contenant les états et empires de la Lune* (1657) were other works of this nature, while Defoe's *Robinson Crusoe* (1719), written seven years before *Gulliver's Travels*, put the traveller's tale into the form of a realistic novel. Traveller's tales of his own time were also parodied by Swift, notable William Dampier's *A New Voyage Round the World* (1657) and *A Voyage to New Holland* (1713–19).

The *Travels* appeal to the reader on many levels. There is the simple attraction of the story. It is funny, it is filled with ingenious invention, and it is exciting. Swift used a literary genre in order to criticize his contemporaries, and he also produced profound comments on human life in general. The story shows us humanity from four different points of view. In the first book Gulliver, among the Lilliputians, sees mankind as ridiculously small. In the second book he is himself minute in comparison with the Brobdingnagians. For instance, when Gulliver was brought home by the farmer and shown to his wife she screamed and ran back 'as women in England do at the sight of a Toad or a Spider'. He was terrified by fear of falling off their thirty foot high table, and disgusted by the sight of a nurse with a monstrous breast feeding a Brobdingnagian baby. In the third book the absurdity of human activities was seen from a common-sensical attitude, the whole book being a species of science fiction in its attitude to time, its mockery of philosophical belief in progress, its dislike of government by experts, its mockery of experimental science. The fourth book describes rational animals, the Houyhnhnms; they regard mankind as irrational, as bestial as the Yahoos. Swift, as he wrote to Pope in 1725, had 'got Materials Towards a Treatis proving the falsity of that Definition *animal rationale*; and to show it should be only *rationis capax*. Upon this great foundation of Misanthropy (though Timon's manner) the whole building of my Travells is erected' (*Corr.*, iii, 103). Since he considered man capable of reason but not a rational creature (like the Houyhnhnms) Swift did not hate mankind as has sometimes been alleged, indeed as he also wrote to Pope 'it is *vous autres* who hate them because you would have them reasonable Animals, and are angry for being disappointed'. (*Corr.*, iii, 118).

We need to remember, as we read the *Travels*, that Gulliver is not Swift; he is an invented character, and not always an admirable one. He himself is an object as much as an instrument of satire. This is true also of the characters in the first voyage, though there are different views on how the allegory is to be worked out in terms of English politics in the early eighteenth century. For example, Sir Charles Firth and A. E. Case have offered different identifications of the ministers at the Lilliputian Court; and scholars have theorized at length on the likely identity of Bolgolam, and Reldresal and on whether Flimnap, the Court Treasurer who is the most expert at a rope dance, is Sir Robert Walpole or perhaps Godolphin. It is easier for the general reader to realize that the High heels, the majority party, are the Tories, and the Low heels, favoured by the Emperor, the Whigs. The religious parties, the Big Endians and the Little Endians (who break their eggs at the large or the small end respectively) represent the Catholics and the Protestants, and while Lilliput is obviously England, Blefescu resembles France.

The Lilliputians are cruel and gradually their treacherous nature is revealed, as we can see them (and, of course, human vice and stupidity) from a detached distance. But the tables are turned in Brobdingnag where our human weaknesses become obvious in relation to the giants and the crude insensitivity of some of them. There are exceptions to this, for Glumdalclitch is consistently kind to Gulliver and the King expresses his horror at European modes of life and the corruptions of Gulliver's society. Though the King is also kind, taking Gulliver into his hands and stroking him gently, his comment on the historical account Gulliver has given him of the politics of Europe in the last century is one of revulsion, 'protesting it was only an Heap of Conspiracies, Rebellions, Murders, Massacres, Revolutions, Banishments; the very worst Effects that Avarice, Rage, Madness, Hatred, Envy, Lust, Malice, and Ambition could produce'. The King continues

'As for yourself . . . who have spent the greatest part of your Life in travelling; I am well disposed to hope you may hitherto have escaped many vices of your country. But, by what I have gathered from your own Relation, and the Answers I have with much Pains wringed and extorted from you; I cannot but conclude the Bulk of your Natives, to be the most pernicious Race of little

26

odious Vermin that Nature ever suffered to crawl upon the Surface of the Earth.'

Gulliver found the physical presence of the Brobdingnagians repulsive, but his attempt to ingratiate himself with the king by giving him an account of gunpowder and offering to build cannon for him was received with intellectual horror:

He was amazed how so impotent and groveling an Insect as I (these were his Expressions) could entertain such inhuman Ideas, and in so familiar a Manner as to appear wholly unmoved at all the Scenes of Blood and Desolation, which I had painted as the Common Effect of those destructive Machines, whereof he said, some evil Genius, Enemy to Mankind, must have been the first Contriver.

And he commanded Gulliver as he valued for his life never to mention this secret any more.

Swift enjoyed himself in parodying the scientists and projectors of the Royal Society in his account of the grand Academy of Lagado in the third book; he mocked the experiments on animals (blood transfusion had been unsuccessfully performed on a dog, and Swift recounts an experiment of deflating and inflating a dog's intestines by the insertion of a bellows in its anus—'the Dog died on the Spot, and we left the Doctor endeavouring to recover him by the same operation') as well as current theories of language. The flying island anticipated science fiction. And for sheer horror little can match the depressing account of the Struldbrugs, immortal, yet regarded as dead in law after eighty, forgetful. 'They were not only opinionative, peevish, covetous, morose, vain, talkative, but uncapable of Friendship and dead to all natural affection ... Beside the usual Deformities in extreme old Age, they acquired an additional Ghastliness in Proportion to their Number of Years, which is not to be described ...'

It is the fourth book of the *Travels* which has caused most critical ink to be spilt. Here Swift splits human qualities between the Houyhnhnms and the Yahoos, the former rational, benevolent, the latter brutish, selfish. The argument is not complete, for we see an occasional comic view of the horses, though Gulliver treats them with respect and reverence, accepting their view of him as a Yahoo, yet trying to meet their approval and his own self-approval by imitating 'their gait and gesture which is now grown into a *H*abit, and my Friends often tell me in a blunt Way, that I *trot like a Horse*; which, however, I take for a great compliment: Neither shall I disown, that in speaking I am apt to fall into the Voice and manner of the *Houyhnhnms*, and hear my self ridiculed on that Account without the least Mortification.'

Gulliver is banished from the Houyhnhnms' island by the horses and when he returns—saved by a benevolent and truly Christian Portuguese captain, Don Pedro, who persuaded him that his duty is to return to his family—we are given Swift's complex ironic attitude to his relatively simple creation.

As soon as I entered the House, my Wife took me in her Arms, and kissed me; at which, having not been used to the Touch of that odious Animal for so many Years, I fell in a Swoon for almost an Hour. At the Time I am writing, it is five Years since my last Return to *England*: During the first Year I could not endure my Wife or Children in my Presence, the very Smell of them was intolerable; much less could I suffer them to eat in the same Room. To this Hour they dare not presume to touch my Bread, or drink out of the same Cup; neither was I ever able to let one of them take me by the Hand. The first money I laid out was to buy two young Stone-Horses, which I keep in a good Stable, and next to them the Groom is my greatest Favourite; for I feel my Spirits revived by the Smell he contracts in the Stable. My horses understand me tolerably well; I converse with them at least four Hours every day.

In the last chapter we realize that Gulliver is himself suffering from what he attacks in others, pride. He is over-simplistic: and his misanthropy and misogyny are absurd. Swift's own view of humanity is larger, ultimately, than the rational satiric view of man Gulliver put forward in his *Travels*.

III.   TORY PROPAGANDA IN ENGLAND AND
HISTORICAL WRITINGS

Swift was well received in London by the new largely Tory cabinet, led by Robert Harley and Henry St John, in 1710. His apprehensions about the future position of the Anglican church after the Whigs' Toleration Act of 1689 had been expressed in *The Sentiments of a Church-of-England Man* (1704), *An Argument to Prove that the Abolishing of Christianity in England, May, as Things Stand, be Attended with some Inconveniences* (1708) and *A Project for the Advancement of Religion and the Reformation of Manners* (1709). His ability to write matched what Harley told Swift was the great difficulty of the new ministry, 'the want of some good pen, to keep up the spirit raised in the people, to assert the principles, and justify the proceedings of the new ministers'. And so from November 1710 onwards Swift wrote for *The Examiner* those pungent and persuasive articles which had such an effect on a small though highly influential readership. The gentry, the clergy, business and professional men were generally tired of the war against France and the taxes raised for it; they were suspicious of the Whigs' attitude to the Anglican Church; they feared for the position of the crown. There was a rift between landed and financial interests. It was obvious to Swift, and he made it equally clear to his readers:

Let any man observe the equipages in this town; he shall find the greater number who make a figure, to be a species of man quite different from any that were ever known before the Revolution, consisting either of Generals or Colonels, or of such whose whole fortunes lie in funds and stocks: so that power, which according to the old maxim, was used to follow land, is now gone over to money.

The only answer to a situation where, as Swift put it, 'through the contrivance and cunning of stockjobbers, there has been brought in such a complication of knavery and cozenage, such a mystery of iniquity, and such an unintelligible jargon of terms to involve it in, as were never known in any other age or country of the world; was the conclusion of a peace'. And Swift's *Examiner* of 23 November 1710 attacked the Duke of Marlborough, 'the great Commander', and also his wealth. In December he turned to Marlborough's request for lifetime employment in the post of Captain-General. This, he argued, was criminal. The *Examiner* was most influential, but it had served its purpose by July 1711. The delicate secret negotiations for peace went on, jealousies had developed between Harley and St John, Marlborough had to be deceived into thinking the war could be prosecuted. Swift returned to England during the height of Grub Street pamphleteering when the secret negotiations had reached their climax, and then his pamphlet *The Conduct of the Allies and of the Late Ministry in Beginning and Carrying on the Present War* was published on 27 November 1711. This devastating attack on Marlborough put forward a conspiratorial view, that the war had been a deception practised by Marlborough and the Whigs:

We have been fighting to raise the wealth and grandeur of a particular family; to enrich usurers and stockjobbers; and to cultivate the pernicious design of a faction by destroying the Landed Interest. The nation begins to think these blessings are not worth fighting for any longer, and therefore desires a peace.

The pamphlet had an immediate effect, and further editions carried its message to more and more readers; it culminated in Marlborough's dismissal on the last day of the year, and this led the way to the Peace of Utrecht. Swift recorded the Captain-General's fall in 'The Widow and Her Cat'; he respected the achievements of Marlborough, despite his own detestation of war. The whole story is one of the power of the printed word, and, as Winston Churchill pointed out in his life of Marlborough, those 'were not days when public men could afford to disdain the Press'.

The Tory ministry, despite Swift's efforts to patch up some peace between Oxford and Bolingbroke, appeared to be doomed. Swift thought 'A Ship's Crew quarelling in a Storm, or while their Enemies are within gun shott' was but a 'faint Idea of this fatal Infatuation'. So he wrote *Some Free Thoughts upon the Present State of Affairs* (1714) which supported St John's policies. Swift's last statements of the Tory point of view were *The History of the Four Last Years of Queen Anne* and his *Memoirs Relating to that Change which happened in Queen Anne's Ministry in the year 1710*, but the death of the Queen, who had thwarted his ambition of preferment in England, brought in George I and the Whigs. To his historical writings Swift brought a firm belief, reinforced by Temple's experience and views, that history depended upon individuals, and a firm conviction that divine intervention could, no matter how hopeless the position of Church and State, alter the history of England. He possessed a superb historical perspective, his knowledge of the past illuminated, he believed, his attitude to the present, and his desire to get the record straight by preserving facts was part of his historiographical method.

IV.   IRISH ANTI-COLONIAL WRITINGS

Swift returned to Ireland to become Dean of St Patrick's Cathedral in 1713: twenty years later he referred to the greatest unhappiness of his life 'I mean, my banishment to this miserable country'. Not only did he miss his literary friends in London—Pope, Prior, Arbuthnot and Gay; not only did he regret not being virtually at the centre of political power, but he disliked being, in effect, a colonial, in 'wretched Dublin, in miserable Ireland'. He had earlier recorded his feelings in *The Story of the Injured Lady*, written in 1707 but not published till after his death. In this he had deplored the effect of English legislation on Ireland, particularly on the Irish wool trade. The 'injured lady' (Ireland) alleges she has been undone by the gentleman (England), 'half by Force and half by Consent after Solemn Vows and Protestations of Marriage': she has been jilted in favour of an inferior rival (Scotland). The Act of Union of 1707 between England and Scotland was something many of the governing Anglo-Irish would then have wished repeated in a union between England and Ireland. Swift's answer to Ireland's plight was that since the gentleman had got possession of her person, obliged her to place her estate under the management of his servants, and reduced her and her tenants to poverty, she should act legally, have the same stewart (*e.g.*, the king) and regulate her household 'by such methods as you shall both agree to'. This stems from the ideas of William Molyneux, an Irish MP, whose *The Case of Ireland being bound by Acts of Parliament in England, Stated* (1698) had put the view that Ireland had its own parliament and owed allegiance to the king, but not to the parliament at Westminster. Swift also argued that Ireland should assert her rights to export her goods where she wished, and he attacked the appointment of Englishmen to office in Ireland.

During Swift's first years in the Deanery he had no wish to play any part in Irish politics, but in 1720 his *Proposals for the Universal Use of Irish Manufacture* . . . put the case for using Irish goods and avoiding importation from England, which had restricted Irish trade. He had much sympathy with the plight of the Dublin weavers, though he thought that Ireland had the right remedies to hand if she would use them. His polemical style had lost none of its force:

the fable, in *Ovid*, of *Arachne* and *Pallas*, is to this Purpose. The Goddess had heard of one *Arachne*, a young Virgin, very famous for *Spinning* and *Weaving*: They both met upon a Tryal of Skill; and *Pallas* finding herself almost equalled in her own Art, stung with Rage and Envy, knockt her *Rival* down, turned her into a *Spyder*, enjoining her to *spin* and *weave* for ever, *out of her own Bowels*, and *in a very narrow Compass*. I confess, that from a Boy, I always pitied poor *Arachne*, and could never heartily love the Goddess, on account of so *cruel and unjust a Sentence*; which, however, is *fully executed* upon *Us* by *England*, with further Additions of *Rigor* and *Severity*. For the greatest part of our *Bowels* and *Vitals* is extracted, without allowing us the Liberty of *spinning* and *weaving* them.

The government prosecuted the printer, but though this prosecution was dropped, the pamphlet did not have much direct success. Swift entered the fray again, when there seemed some chance of rallying and encouraging opposition to a patent granted to an English ironmaster, William Wood, in July 1722, to allow him to coin copper money for Ireland. The Irish Privy Council, the Lords Justice, the Commissioners of Revenue and the two Irish houses of Parliament had declared against the patent, and Swift made devastating attacks on the project, adopting the *persona* of a Dublin shopkeeper, M. B. Drapier, in a series of letters, the first of which was entitled *A Letter to the Shop-Keepers, Tradesmen, Farmers, and Common-People of Ireland*, while the fourth was addressed to 'the Whole People of Ireland'. By this phrase Swift probably meant the Irish protestant 'garrison'; in his own words, the 'true English people of Ireland'; those whom he was to describe in a letter to Pope of June 1737 as 'the English gentry of this kingdom' as opposed to the 'savage old Irish'. While arguing that the people of Ireland are and ought to be as free a people as their brethren in England ('Am I a *Free-Man* in *England*, and do I become a *Slave* in Six Hours by crossing Channel?'), attacking the theory that Ireland was '*a depending kingdom*', and destroying any credibility which might have attached to Wood's coinage, he was creating an active public opinion, and in September 1725 it was announced that Wood's patent had been withdrawn. Swift had become a popular Irish hero, an Irish patriot.

Irish affairs, however, despite the defeat of Wood's coinage, did not greatly change, as the pessimistic attitude which permeates *A Short View of the State of Ireland* (1727–8) indicated. There followed a series of bad harvests—'three years dearth of corn, and every place strowed with beggars . . . the kingdom is absolutely undone', as Swift described the situation to Pope in a letter of 11 August 1729—and his sense of horror is recorded in what is perhaps the most stirring satire. *A Modest Proposal for Preventing the Children of the Poor in Ireland from being Burdensome, and for making them Beneficial* (1729). In this he argues his case as if he were an economist, putting forward his politico-economic project coolly and reasonably, with statements of the situation and some persuasive statistics. His appeal to the reader on moral grounds makes his suggestion for a solution of the Irish problem the more devastating when he reveals it in a matter-of-fact manner:

I have been assured by a very knowing *American* of my Acquaintance in *London*; that a young healthy Child, well nursed, is, at a Year old, a most delicious, nourishing and wholesome Food: whether *Stewed, Roasted, Baked,* or *Boiled*; and, I make no doubt, that it will equally serve in a *fricasie*, or *Ragoust*.

The scheme is carefully calculated:

I do therefore humbly offer it to *publick Consideration* that of the Hundred and Twenty Thousand Children already computed, Twenty thousand may be reserved for Breed . . . That the remaining Hundred thousand may, at a Year old, be offered in Sale to the

33

Persons of Quality and *Fortune*, through the Kingdom; always advising the Mothers to let them suck plentifully in the last Month, so as to render them plump and fat for a good Table.

The *Modest Proposal* records Swift's disgust with the poverty of Ireland, but he thought that Irish apathy and selfishness and greed created it as much as English policy. His *saeva indignatio*, his fierce indignation, emerges through his scathingly ironic use of metaphor:

I grant this food will be somewhat dear, and therefore very *proper for Landlords*; who, as they have already devoured most of the parents, seem to have the best title to the children.

V. THE PROSE STYLE AND SWIFT'S SATIRE

In *Gulliver's Travels* Swift wrote of the style of the Brobdingnagians which he described as 'clear, masculine and smooth but not florid; for they avoid nothing more than multiplying unnecessary words, or using various expressions'. This description could be applied to his own writing after *A Tale of a Tub* where he had allowed his sense of comedy, irreverence, and particularly parody, its head. He became deeply disturbed about the degeneration of the English language in his own day; he thought the peaceable part of King Charles I's reign was the time when English was at its best. This was very different from the attitude of those who had altered English for the purposes of scientific communication, those who had produced the close naked speech praised by Sprat in his history of the Royal Society. Swift thought that

During the Usurpation, Such an Infusion of Enthusiastick Jargon prevailed in every Writing, as was not shaken off in many Years after. To this succeeded that Licentiousness which entered with the *Restoration*; and from infecting on Religion and Morals, fell to corrupt our Language: Which last was not like to be much improved by those who, at that Time, make up the Court of King Charles the Second; either such who had followed him in

34

his Banishment, or who had been altogether conversant in the Dialect of those *Fanatick Times*.

Swift tended to associate language with history, with politics, with religion. He wrote on English in *The Tatler* (number 280, 1710) and his *Proposal for Correcting, Improving and Ascertaining the English Tongue* (1712), his *Letter to a Young Gentleman* (1719–1720), his *Complete Collection of Genteel and Ingenious Conversation* (1738) show his concern with language. For his political purposes, for his pamphlets, he needed a middle style, which would, in effect, avoid the extremes of decadent courtier or disloyal dissenter, of licentiousness and fanaticism. He thought that an academy, founded on the example of the French Academy, might act prescriptively, to define correct English and fix it—a thing we now think virtually impossible to achieve. But for him language was not only associated with history, politics and religion: it was part and parcel of morality as he saw it. So clarity was to be sought above all: 'propriety and correctness of speech'. What this meant in his case was the right word in the right place. He distrusted rhetoric which appealed to passion: his own plain style was none the less rhetorical, designed to provoke, to vex, to rouse. He translated arguments into literal terms; he pursued them to their limits. He was aware of his audience; he offered it concrete examples which could be understood. He is said to have summoned his servants, had his proofs read aloud to them, and then to have altered his writing until the servants fully understood it. He aimed, then, not only at the educated classes but at ordinary intelligent people; he had therefore to use an English which was, above all, normal; that is to say uneccentric, commonplace, simple and generally acceptable, a prose which could evoke decent, tolerant responses, and which, could, paradoxically, provide a vehicle for what is perhaps his main contribution to English literature, his departure from the normal, the peculiarly powerful irony which carried his satire so effectively.

Satire in Swift's hands was a great cleansing force: it shifted the rubbish, it cut clear channels through the corruption of his own day—the hypocrisy and cant, the sheer stupidity and dullness of many of his contemporaries—and it remains with us, for the things he attacked are with us still. He was profoundly aware of the absurdities of human life, he found injustice and irrationality revolting, he dwelt with disgust upon the ugly, unhygienic aspects of eighteenth-century life; and yet he had two main approaches; he described one as lashing vice; the other was ridiculing. The latter was natural for 'a man of mirth' as many of his friends saw him, exuberant in his invention and sense of comic absurdity.

He could rail directly at the men whom he distrusted or disliked: this kind of satire runs the risk of seeming abusive or crude and his other methods stand the test of time better. His indirect methods of irony led him into impersonating his enemies, or achieving his effects indirectly with a dead-pan style, or else by either diminishing or inflating an enemy's argument. And there was his habit of shifting his style from the reasonable and urbane to the disturbingly violent. He could also surprise his readers by omitting normal or expected human qualities, notably, for instance, in *A Modest Proposal* which avoids any humanitarian sense of pity. This is part of one of his techniques, of being allusive, or forcing the reader to face for himself the problems presented by the printed word. In short, his methods possessed immense variety, informed by that intensity of feeling he brought to bear on the temporary and the lasting issues of his age. The imperishable qualities of his satire are in part achieved by the quality of his imagination which imbued his inventions with the quality of fact, and of reality, and therefore, even now, with that of convincing contemporaneity.

VI. THE POETRY

Swift's poetry has an engaging directness: he wrote occasional poems to amuse himself and others, to pay tribute and to denigrate, to capture details of the life about him, and to justify himself. He regarded his verses as written 'upon trifles' though they were never composed 'without a moral view'; trifles they may have seemed to him, but the total impact of his poetry gives us insight into the way his mind worked, shows us his skill with words (the fun he got out of punning and out of rhyming, not always very precisely) as well as his sense of realism. In the 'Ode to Mr Congreve' he offered advice:

> *Beat not the dirty paths where vulgar feet have trod*
> *But give the vigorous fancy room*

And he took his own advice to heart. His fancy played with a wide range of subjects, and he could parody well-trodden, heroic or pastoral paths with acute irony, as well as adapting classical models, notably poems of Horace, to his own uses.

What beats through all his verse, even the early Odes, is the accent of very direct speech. The formal structure of the Pindaric Ode which he used in his early poems was not completely suitable, in his kind of poetry, yet in the 'Ode to Sir William Temple' he contrived to convey his genuine respect and at the close of that poem to express his own feelings. Nature, he says, has tied him to the Muse's galleys:

> In vain I strive to cross this spacious main,
> In vain I try and pull the oar
> And when I almost reach the shore
> Strait the Muse turns the helm, and I launch out again;
>   And yet to feed my pride,
> Whene'er I mourn, stops my complaining breath
> With promise of a mad reversion after death.

He offered Temple the tribute of a humbler Muse

> Nature the hidden spark did at my birth infuse
> And kindled first with Indolence and Ease,
> And since too oft debauch'd by praise,
> 'Tis now grown an incurable Disease:
> In vain to quench this foolish fire I try
> In Wisdom and Philosophy;
> In vain all wholesome Herbs I sow,
> Where nought but weeds will grow.
> Whate'er I plant (like Corn on barren Earth)
> By an equivocal Birth
> Seeds and runs up to Poetry.

This should be contrasted with a poem of 1735, 'On poetry: a rhapsody' which exhibits an old man's frenzy:

> Not Beggar's Brat, on Bulk begot;
> Not Bastard of a Pedlar *Scot*;
> Not Boy brought up to cleaning shoes,
> The Spawn of Bridewell, or the Stews;
> Not Infants dropt, the spurious Pledges
> Of Gipsies littering under Hedges,
> Are so disqualified by Fate
> To rise in *Church* or Law, or State,
> As he, whom Phebus in his Ire
> Hath blasted with poetick Fire.

These early Odes show his desire to get below surface appearances: they contain his fierce awareness of human mortality. For him poetry was a means of clarifying, even of condensing experience, of arriving at truth. But it had to seem casual, paradoxically both concise and conversational, direct and clear. Thus in two poems, 'A Description of the Morning' and 'A Description of a City Shower' (both published in *The Tatler* in 1710, numbers 9 and 238 respectively), he gave an impression of movement and noise, assembling details together into a general and convincing pattern of city life, ironically mocking in the process aspects of heroic and pastoral poetry. The rhythm and the rhymes give an urgency to the lines on the shower:

> Now from all Parts the swelling Kennels flow,
> And bear their Trophies with them go:
> Filth of all Hues and Odours seem to tell
> What Streets they sailed from, by the Sight and Smell.
> They, as each Torrent drives, with rapid Force
> From *Smithfield*, or *St Pulchre's* shape their Course,
> And in huge Confluent join at *Snow-Hill Ridge*,
> Fall from the *Conduit* prone to *Holborn-Bridge*.
> Sweepings from Butchers Stalls, Dung, Guts, and Blood,
> Drown'd Puppies, stinking Sprats, all drench'd in Mud,
> Dead Cats and Turnip-Tops come tumbling down the
>   Flood.

Here Swift is insisting upon the crude reality of ordinary objects. Human attitudes to life he captured equally well in

the speech he created in colloquial monologues—the famous
'Humble Petition of Frances Harris' (1710) with all its
breathless account of the loss of her money.

Now you must know because my Trunk has a very bad lock
Therefore all the Money, I have, which, *God* knows, is a
                                        very small stock,
I keep in a Pocket ty'd about my Middle, next my smock.
So when I went to put up my Purse, as *God* would have it,
                                        my smock was unript,
And, instead of putting it into my Pocket, down it slipt . . .

And the poem moves to her real problem, the possible loss of
the Chaplain as a husband. No less effective is a later poem in
this genre 'Mary the Cook-Maid's Letter to Mr Sheridan'
(1718) which captures the rattling speech of a forthright
Irish servant.
    Swift adopted octosyllabic couplets, and in so doing found
the right form for expressing himself. The directness and
control of his lines is noteworthy. He wrote some political
poems during his stay in London: these lampoons were
clever, notably the attack on Marlborough in 'A Fable of the
Widow and her Cat' or 'The Virtues of Sid Hamett the
magician's Rod' (1726) on Lord Godolphin. He continued
his attack on Marlborough even after his death in 'A Satyrical
Elegy on the Death of a late famous general':

    Let pride be taught by this rebuke
    How very mean a thing's a Duke
    From all his ill-got Honours flung
    Turn'd to that dirt from whence he sprung.

These poems chimed with his political prose, and later, when
he was involved in combating Wood's halfpence with
The Drapier's Letters, his poems (of 1724–5) again displayed
a satiric liveliness of invention, a vitality of interpretation,
which emerged in the bursting vigour of 'Mad Mullinix and
Timothy' (1728) and 'A Character Panegyric and Description
of the Legion Club' (1736), a comment on the Irish Parliament, matched only by the bitter view expressed in 'Ireland'
(1727).

Before Swift settled in Dublin as Dean of St Patrick's he wrote *Cadenus and Vanessa,* his longest poem, in 889 lines, an account of his relationship (Cadenus is an anagram of *Decanus,* Latin for Dean) with Esther Vanhomrigh. This poem contrasts Vanessa's perfections and the imperfections of contemporary women which correspond to the failings of society, by means of setting this moral fable in a mythological setting where the two sexes dispute before Venus. The poem tells of Cadenus's surprise at Vanessa's falling in love with him:

> *Vanessa,* not in Years a Score
> Dreams of a Gown of forty-four;
> Imaginary Charms can find,
> In Eyes with Reading almost blind;
> *Cadenus* now no more appears
> Declin'd in Health, advanc'd in Years.
> She fancies Musick in his Tongue
> Nor further looks but thinks him Young.

He is flattered, but his dignity and age forbid him to engage in love:

> But friendship in its greatest Height,
> A constant, rational Delight,
> On Virtue's Basis fix'd to last,
> When Love's allurements long are past;
> Which gently warms but cannot burn;
> He gladly offers in return.

Vanessa sees the situation of pupil and tutor is reversed:

> But what success Vanessa met,
> Is to the world a Secret yet:
> Whether the Nymph to please her Swain,
> Talks in a high Romantick Strain;
> Or whether he at last descends
> To like with less Seraphick Ends;
> Or, to compound the Business, whether
> They temper Love and Books together;
> Must never to Mankind be told,
> Nor shall the conscious Muse unfold.

The poem pays its compliments to Vanessa, but the interest for us is its autobiographical account of the problems of one of Swift's close relationships. The other, Swift's friendship with Stella, gave rise to revealing poems, some written for her birthdays, in which he paid tribute to her character, her intelligence and her care for him. In these he pays her compliments ('On Stella's Birthday, written 1718–19'), praises her kindness ('To Stella, visiting me in my Sickness'), stresses their friendship

> Thou *Stella* wert no longer young
> When first for thee my Harp I strung;
> Without one Word of Cupid's Darts,
> Of killing Eyes, or bleeding Hearts:
> With Friendship and Esteem possesst,
> I ne'er admitted Love a guest
> > ('To Stella, who collected and Transcribed
> > his Poems')

Other poems stress the lasting quality of her intellect ('Stella's Birthday' written AD 1720–21), tease her ('Stella's Distress on the 3rd fatal day of October 1723', rewritten as 'Stella at Wood-Park') when she finds her Dublin lodgings small after staying at Wood Park, praise her for missing him on her birthday—a self-pitying poem ('To Stella . . . written on the day of her Birth, but not on the Subject when I was sick in Bed') in his being 56, she 43 ('Stella's Birthday, 1725'), on her being too thin ('A receipt to restore Stella's youth', written in the Year 1724–5) and, perhaps the most moving of all, as Stella was dying in 1727:

> This Day whate'er the fates decree,
> Shall still be kept with Joy by me:
> This Day then, let us not be told,
> That you are sick and I grown old,
> Nor think on our approaching ills,
> And talk of Spectacles and Pills;
> To morrow will be time enough
> To hear such mortifying stuff.
> Yet since from Reason may be brought
> A better and more pleasing thought,
> Which can in spite of all Decays
> Support a few remaining Days:

From not the gravest of Divines,
Accept for once some serious lines
Although we now can form no more
Fond schemes of Life, as here to fore;
Yet you, while Time is running fast,
Can look with Joy on what is past . . .

Perhaps the deepest sign of his care for Stella is to be found in
'Holyhead, September 25, 1717', the moody, angry poem he
wrote when, deeply anxious about her 'On whom my fears
and hopes depend', he was held up by contrary winds:

Lo here I sit at holy head
With muddy ale and mouldy bread
All Christian vittals stink of fish
I'm where my enemies would wish . . .

Swift's last poems returned to his basic interest in the
difference between truth and illusion. 'The Problem', a poem
of 1699, had dealt with the animal side of love, and such
poems as 'The Lady's Dressing Room' (1732) stressed his
loathing of untidiness and lack of hygiene. 'A beautiful
young nymph going to bed' (1734) developed the attack
on appearance and reality by showing how Erinna dis-
mantles her artificial aids at night while 'Strephon and Chloe'
(1734), describing Strephon's shock at discovering that his
bride was all too human, stressed the need for maintaining
decency.

Swift did not accept a *persona* in poetry as in prose. Thus
his attitude towards himself appeared unequivocally in
several poems. 'The Author upon Himself' (1714) was a
straightforward if ironic account of his life in London, and
his retiring from political life, 'The Life and Character of Dr
Swift' (1731), exhibited a frank desire to weigh up his
achievement, albeit laughingly, but the 'Verses on the Death
of Dr Swift' (1739) had its sadness as it considered how
quickly he will be forgotten. While playing cards the ladies

Receive the news in doleful dumps,
The Dean is dead, (and what is *Trumps?*)
Then Lord have mercy on his Soul
(Ladies I'll venture for the *Vole*)

Six Deans they say must bear the Pall
(I wish I knew what *King* to call) . . .

He defended his satire and his moral view, remarked how he
had exposed the fool and lashed the knave

Yet malice never was his Aim
He lash'd the Vice but spar'd the Name.

And finally, ironically, he linked himself yet again with the
land he hated:

He gave the little Wealth he had,
To build a House for Fools and Mad:
And show'd by one satyric Touch,
No nation wanted it so much.

VII. THE CORRESPONDENCE

Swift's letters have an immediacy about them, they too
reflect his desire to write unaffectedly and intimately, and
they are written in a graphic, lively style. He provided his
recipients with what he might have offered them in conversation. Thus he seems to talk out loud to Stella and her
friend Rebecca Dingley in the *Journal to Stella*, the letters he
wrote them from London. He returns from his days among
the great and relaxes in telling the ladies in Dublin the events
of his day in London, as well as relaying the gossip of the
town. From them we can piece together his care over
money, coupled with his generosity, his fiery independence,
his desire to be treated like a lord. He could tell Stella how he
called on the Secretary St John, and told him 'never to appear
cold to me, for I would not be treated like a school boy'.
St John 'took all right; said I had reason' and would have had
Swift dine with him 'to make up matters; but I would not.
I don't know, but I would not.' Stella knew him well; he had
taught her to despise the shows of the world, so to her he
could recount his sorrows—the death of Lady Ashburnham,
for instance; he could scold her and tease her, and demand
from her news of his garden in Ireland, of his fruit trees and
willows and the trout stream.

Swift emerges from these letters in all his complexity, coarse and sensitive, proud yet ready to serve; humanly despairing and yet ready to endure. To Stella he could be imperious and instructive, gay and scathing, tender and scathing, tender and tolerant. We hear of his health, his troubles with servants, his forebodings about the government.

In letters to others we learn of his domestic situation, as Dean in Dublin, for instance, often depressed by the effects of Ménière's Disease, yet energetically taking vast exercise. There is one charming vignette:

I often ride out in fair weather, with one of my servants laden with a Joynt of meat and a bottle of wine, and Town bread, who attends me to some rural parson 5 or 6 miles round this Town.

There were many letters to Archbishop King, filled with the latest political views, yet discreet, for he knew well the man to whom he was writing. There were the letters to his younger friend Charles Ford, and the jesting punning letters to Sheridan. Swift wrote many letters: and through them, as through his poems, there runs a nimbleness and drive, whether he is dispensing a moral view, or enjoying some piece of raillery. The taut language of his letters reinforces his desire for simplicity; they are always concise. They range from statesmanship to literary satire; to his friends he showed his jocosity, his natural inventiveness, and, at times, his moods of deep depression.

He fought for health. There is a touching letter to Charles Ford advising him to take exercise and be temperate for his health's sake. In this Swift argues that life is not of much value but health is everything. For his part, he wrote, he laboured for daily health 'as often and almost as many hours as a workman does for daily bread, and like a common labourer can but just earn enough to keep life and soul together'. It was to Ford he wrote that he had finished *Gulliver's Travels* and was transcribing them. As always there is the query of how far to accept his literal meaning, for he commented on them 'they are admirable Things, and will wonderfully mend the World'. And in a letter to Pope he wrote a sentence which does more to explain him than the writings of most commentators

All my endeavours from a boy, to distinguish myself, were only for want of a great title and fortune, that I might be used like a Lord by those who have an opinion of my parts—whether right or wrong, it is no great matter, and so the reputation of wit or great learning does the office of a blue ribbon, or of a coach and six horses.

VIII. THE ULTIMATE ACHIEVEMENT

Lord Bathurst, writing in 1730 of Swift's achievement in his time, summed up his success in words which are still useful:

You have overturned and supported Ministers. You have set Kingdoms in a flame by your pen. Pray, what is there in that but having the knack of hitting the passions of mankind?

A fair comment and query; but it does not solve the problem of the elusive man behind the masks. Swift remains elusive, apt to rouse the passions of his readers into admiration or dislike. The evils of existence, as the late Bonamy Dobrée well put it, are combated with laughter by men such as Swift, who balance their critical, satiric spirits and their savage indignation with an exuberant, fantastic humour. And when there was no need for indignation at the irrationality and injustice of men, when reasonableness prevailed and life ran in smooth social currents, the humour was urbane, teasing where tacit, protective affection existed, creating mirth out of irony, when fierce passions were temporarily lulled. Swift moved between moods, as Vanessa knew to her cost: she recorded how he could shake her with prodigious awe so that she trembled with fear, but at other times her soul was revived by the charming compassion which shone through Swift's soul. His *saeva indignatio* was matched by what Ford called his capacity 'for mirth and society'; and Arbuthnot once wrote that it was not Swift's wit and good conversation that he valued him for, but for being a sincere honest man, and speaking truth when others were afraid to speak it.

45

SWIFT

A Select Bibliography

(Place of publication London, unless stated otherwise. Detailed bibliographical information will also be found in the appropriate volume of
The Cambridge Bibliography of English Literature and *The Oxford History
of English Literature*.)

Bibliography:

A BIBLIOGRAPHY OF THE WRITINGS IN PROSE AND VERSE, by H. Teerink;
The Hague (1937)
—revised edition, edited by A. H. Scouten, Philadelphia, 1963. This
is a comprehensive work, superseding W. S. Jackson's Bibliography
(Vol. XII of *Prose Works*, ed. T. Scott, 1908) and containing
extensive lists of doubtful and supposititious writings as well as of
critical and biographical studies.

CONTRIBUTIONS TOWARDS A BIBLIOGRAPHY OF 'GULLIVER'S TRAVELS', by
L. L. Hubbard (1922).

THE MOTTE EDITIONS OF 'GULLIVER'S TRAVELS', by H. Williams (1925)
—see also Sir H. Williams's authoritative bibliography of the early
editions in his edition of *Gulliver's Travels* (First Edition Club, 1926).

THE REPUTATION OF SWIFT, 1781–1882, by D. M. Berwick; Philadelphia
(1941).

JONATHAN SWIFT: A List of Critical Studies, 1895–1945, compiled by
L. A. Landa and J. E. Tobin; New York (1945)
—a valuable guide to numerous articles in learned journals, with an
account of Swift MSS in American libraries, by D. H. Davis.

THE ROTHSCHILD LIBRARY, 2 vols (1954)
—contains full descriptions of the important collection of printed
books, pamphlets and manuscripts by Swift formed by Lord Rothschild, with references to bibliographical studies of separate works
published since Teerink.

SWIFT AND THE TWENTIETH CENTURY, by M. Voigt; Detroit (1964).

A BIBLIOGRAPHY OF SWIFT STUDIES 1945–1965, compiled by J. J. Stathis;
Nashville, Tennessee (1967).

FAIR LIBERTY WAS ALL HIS CRY, ed. A. Norman Jeffares (1967).
—includes 'A Checklist of Critical and Biographical Writings on
Jonathan Swift, 1945–65', by Claire Lamont.

Collected Works:

MISCELLANIES IN PROSE AND VERSE (1711)
—apart from a 16-page pamphlet (1710), the earliest collection of
Swift's writings. A number of unauthorized and pirated Swiftian

'Miscellanies' of varied content were published during the following quarter of a century.

MISCELLANIES IN PROSE AND VERSE, 3 vols (1727)

—these first three volumes of the 'Swift-Pope Miscellanies' were extended by a fourth volume ('The Third Volume') in 1732 and a fifth in 1735. An edition in 6 volumes, containing some variations appeared in 1736. This famous collection was from the first frequently reprinted and reissued in various combinations of editions and dates. By 1751 it had been extended to 13 volumes.

THE DRAPIER'S MISCELLANY; Dublin (1733)

—miscellaneous pieces in verse and prose relating to the Irish economy.

WORKS, 4 vols; Dublin (1735)

—published by Faulkner, with Swift's tacit approval, this textually important edition was extended to 6 volumes in 1738, to 8 volumes in 1746, to 11 volumes in 1763, and by 1769 to 20 volumes (with the Letters). Sets of the reprinted volumes of various dates are found in irregular combinations.

POETICAL WORKS; Dublin (1736)

—a separate reprint of Vol. II of Faulkner's second edition of the *Works*. A number of separate editions of Swift's poetical works were published during the eighteenth century and his poems were included in the well-known series edited by Bell, Johnson, Anderson, Park, etc.

WORKS, ed. J. Hawkesworth, 6 or 12 vols (1755-75)

—a rival of Faulkner's edition, published simultaneously in 6 volumes 4to and 12 volumes 8vo, 1755, subsequently extended by 8 additional 4to volumes and 13 additional 8vo volumes. Also published later in 27 volumes 18mo.

WORKS, ed. T. Sheridan, 17 vols (1784)

—based on Hawkesworth's text.

WORKS, 19 vols (1801: 24 vols (12mo) 1803)

—Sheridan's edition 'corrected and revised' by J. Nichols.

WORKS, ed. Sir W. Scott, 19 vols; Edinburgh (1814: 2nd ed. 1824; reprinted 1883)

—Vol. I contains Scott's long biographical essay.

PROSE WORKS, ed. T. Scott, 12 vols (1897-1908)

—Vol XII is a Bibliography by W. S. Jackson.

THE DRAPIER'S LETTERS TO THE PEOPLE OF IRELAND AGAINST RECEIVING WOOD'S HALFPENCE, ed. H. Davis; Oxford (1935)

—the definitive edition.

PROSE WORKS, ed. H. Davis, 15 vols; Oxford (1939-64)

—the definitive 'Shakespeare Head' edition, with valuable introductions and bibliographical and textual notes.

POEMS, ed. H. Williams, 3 vols; Oxford (1937)
—the definitive edition; second edition, revised, 1958.
COLLECTED POEMS, ed. J. Horrell, 2 vols (1958)
—in the Muses' Library.

Selected Works:

Among the many selections from Swift's writings, ranging from
school texts to limited editions-de-luxe and including volumes in
such series as Everyman's Library, Collins' Classics, etc., the following are noteworthy: *Satires and Personal Writings* (ed. W. A. Eddy),
1932; *Gulliver's Travels and Selected Prose and Verse* (Nonesuch
Press, ed. J. Hayward), 1934; *Selected Prose Works* (Cresset Library,
ed. J. Hayward), 1949.

Letters:

LETTERS TO AND FROM DR J. SWIFT, 1714–1738; Dublin (1741)
—also published as Vol. VII of Faulkner's edition of *Works*.
LETTERS, ed. J. Hawkesworth (1766).
LETTERS, ed. J. Hawkesworth and D. Swift, 6 vols (1768–9)
—published as part of Hawkesworth's edition of *Works*.
UNPUBLISHED LETTERS, ed. G. B. Hill (1899).
VANESSA AND HER CORRESPONDENCE WITH SWIFT, ed. A. M. Freeman
(1921)
—the first publication of the 'love letters' of Swift and Esther
Vanhomrigh.
LETTERS TO CHARLES FORD, ed. D. Nichol Smith; Oxford (1935)
—edited for the first time from the originals, now for the most part
in the Rothschild Library.
THE JOURNAL TO STELLA, ed. H. Williams, 2 vols; Oxford (1948)
—the definitive edition. The letters to Esther Johnson, comprising
the so-called 'Journal to Stella', were first printed, more or less in-
accurately, in Hawkesworth's *Works*, Vol. X, 1766 (Letters 1 and
41–65) and in Vol. XII, 1768 (Letters 2–40). Later editions: ed.
G. A. Aitken, 1901; ed. F. Ryland (Vol. II of T. Scott's edition of
Works, 1905); ed. J. K. Moorhead, 1924 (Everyman's Library).
THE CORRESPONDENCE OF JONATHAN SWIFT, ed. H. Williams, 5 vols;
Oxford (1963–5).

Separate Works:

Note: This section does not include single pieces printed as broadsides
or as folio half-sheets; contributions to periodicals (e.g. *The Tatler,
The Examiner*), and to books by other writers, for which see *Prose
Works*, ed. H. Davis, and *Poems*, ed. H. Williams; or any of the
numerous doubtful or supposititious works which at various times
have been ascribed to Swift. (For the titles of the latter, see Teerink's

Bibliography and the excellent short-title list by H. Williams in *CBEL*)

A DISCOURSE OF THE CONTESTS AND DISSENSIONS BETWEEN THE NOBLES AND THE COMMONS IN ATHENS AND ROME (1701). *Politics*

A TALE OF A TUB [AND THE BATTLE OF THE BOOKS] (1704). *Polemical Satire*

—annotated edition, with plates, 1710. *The Battle of the Books* was Swift's contribution to the famous Quarrel of the Ancients and the Moderns. The definitive edition of both works was edited by A. Guthkelch and D. Nichol Smith, Oxford, 1920.

PREDICTIONS FOR THE YEAR 1708 (1708). *Parody*

—the first of several jesting satires against almanac-makers (and one, Partridge, in particular), written under the pseudonym of Isaac Bickerstaff during 1708–9.

A PROJECT FOR THE ADVANCEMENT OF RELIGION AND THE REFORMATION OF MANNERS (1709). *Moral Instruction*

A LETTER . . . CONCERNING THE SACRAMENTAL TEST (1709). *Church Politics*

BAUCIS AND PHILEMON (1709). *Verse*

—Swift's first separately printed poem. Reprinted with other poems and with the prose parody, *A Meditation upon a Broom-Stick*, in 1710

THE EXAMINER (1710–11). *Political Journalism*

—32 weekly issues, beginning with No. 14, 26 Oct. 1710, were written by Swift.

A SHORT CHARACTER OF . . . [THE EARL OF WHARTON] (1711). *Invective*

SOME REMARKS UPON A PAMPHLET (1711). *Politics*

A NEW JOURNEY TO PARIS (1711). *Politics*

A LEARNED COMMENT UPON DR HARE'S EXCELLENT SERMON (1711). *Church Politics*

THE CONDUCT OF THE ALLIES (1712[1711]). *Politics*

—the definitive edition was edited, with introduction and notes, by C. B. Wheeler, Oxford, 1916.

SOME ADVICE HUMBLY OFFER'D TO THE MEMBERS OF THE OCTOBER CLUB (1712). *Politics*

SOME REMARKS ON THE BARRIER TREATY (1712). *Politics*

A PROPOSAL FOR CORRECTING . . . THE ENGLISH TONGUE (1712). *Criticism*

SOME REASONS TO PROVE THAT NO PERSON IS OBLIGED BY HIS PRINCIPLES AS A WHIG, ETC. (1712). *Politics*

A LETTER OF THANKS . . . TO THE . . . BISHOP OF S. ASAPH (1712). *Church Politics*

MR C[OLLI]N'S DISCOURSE OF FREE-THINKING (1713). *Polemics*

49

PART OF THE SEVENTH EPISTLE OF THE FIRST BOOK OF HORACE IMITATED (1713). *Verse*

THE IMPORTANCE OF THE GUARDIAN CONSIDERED (1713). *Politics*

THE FIRST ODE OF THE SECOND BOOK OF HORACE PARAPHRAS'D (171[4]). *Verse*

THE PUBLICK SPIRIT OF THE WHIGS (1714). *Politics*

AN ARGUMENT TO PROVE THAT THE ABOLISHING OF CHRISTIANITY IN ENGLAND, ETC. (1717)
—first published in the *Miscellanies*, 1711.

A PROPOSAL FOR THE UNIVERSAL USE OF IRISH MANUFACTURE (1720). *Political Economy*
—*A Defence of English Commodities*, 1720, an answer to this pamphlet, was probably written by Swift.

A LETTER . . . TO A GENTLEMAN DESIGNING FOR HOLY ORDERS (1720). *Criticism*

THE SWEARER'S BANK (1720). *Satire*

THE BUBBLE (1721). *Verse*

A LETTER OF ADVICE TO A YOUNG POET; Dublin (1721). *Criticism*
—long ascribed to Swift but probably not by him.

SOME ARGUMENTS AGAINST ENLARGING THE POWER OF THE BISHOPS (1723). *Church Politics*

A LETTER TO THE SHOP-KEEPERS (1724). *Political Economy*
—the first of the celebrated 'Drapier's Letters'.

A LETTER TO MR HARDING THE PRINTER (1724). *Political Economy*
—the second of the 'Drapier's Letters'.

SOME OBSERVATIONS UPON A PAPER (1724). *Political Economy*
—the third of the 'Drapier's Letters'.

A LETTER TO THE WHOLE PEOPLE OF IRELAND (1724). *Political Economy*
—the fourth of the 'Drapier's Letters'.

A LETTER TO . . . VISCOUNT MOLESWORTH (1724). *Political Economy*
—the fifth and last of the 'Drapier's Letters'. They were published together in Dublin in 1725 as *Fraud Detected: or, the Hibernian Patriot*. The definitive edition of the *Drapier's Letters* was edited by H. Davis; Oxford, 1935.

THE BIRTH OF MANLY VIRTUE (1725). *Verse*

CADENUS AND VANESSA: A Poem (1726). *Verse*

[GULLIVER'S] TRAVELS INTO SEVERAL REMOTE NATIONS OF THE WORLD, 2 vols (1726). *Satirical Fantasy*
—Faulkner's text (*Works*, 1735, Vol. III), which was revised with Swift's co-operation, was first reprinted in modern times in the 'Nonesuch' *Swift*, and later in the Cresset Library *Swift*, in the 'Shakespeare Head' *Swift* (Vol. XI), and in Collins' Classics. The definitive edition of the text of the first edition of 1726 was

elaborately edited by H. Williams for the First Edition Club in 1926.

A SHORT VIEW OF THE STATE OF IRELAND; Dublin (1727–8). *Political Economy*

AN ANSWER TO A PAPER CALLED 'A MEMORIAL OF THE POOR INHABITANTS'; Dublin (1728). *Political Economy*

THE INTELLIGENCER; Dublin (1728). *Political Journalism*
—20 weekly numbers by Swift and Sheridan. Published as a volume in 1729. No. 19 was printed separately in 1736 as *A Letter . . . to a Country Gentleman in the North of Ireland*.

A MODEST PROPOSAL; Dublin (1729). *Sociological Satire*

THE JOURNAL OF A DUBLIN LADY; Dublin (1729). *Verse*
—reprinted in London as *The Journal of a Modern Lady*.

A PANEGYRIC ON . . . DEAN SWIFT; Dublin (1729–30). *Verse*

AN EPISTLE TO . . . LORD CARTERET; Dublin (1730). *Politics*

AN EPISTLE UPON AN EPISTLE; Dublin (1730). *Verse*

A LIBEL ON D[OCTOR] D[ELANY] (1730). *Verse*

A VINDICATION OF . . . LORD CARTERET (1730). *Politics*

TRAULUS [Two parts, Dublin] (1730). *Verse*

HORACE, BOOK I: ODE XIV [Dublin] ([17]30). *Verse*

A SOLDIER AND A SCHOLAR (1732). *Verse*
—reprinted (Dublin, 1732) as *The Grand Question Debated*.

CONSIDERATIONS UPON TWO BILLS (1732). *Church Politics*

AN EXAMINATION OF CERTAIN ABUSES; Dublin (1732). *Sociological Satire*
—the title of the London edition (1732) begins: *City Cries, Instrumental and Vocal*.

THE LADY'S DRESSING ROOM (1732). *Verse*

THE ADVANTAGES PROPOSED BY REPEALING THE SACRAMENTAL TEST; Dublin (1732). *Church Politics*

AN ELEGY ON DICKY AND DOLLY; Dublin (1732). *Verse*

THE LIFE AND GENUINE CHARACTER OF DOCTOR SWIFT. WRITTEN BY HIMSELF (1733). *Verse*

ON POETRY: A Rapsody (1733). *Verse*

THE PRESBYTERIANS' PLEA OF MERIT; Dublin (1733). *Church Politics*

SOME REASONS AGAINST THE BILL FOR SETTLING THE TYTH OF HEMP BY A MODUS; Dublin (1734). *Political Economy*

AN EPISTLE TO A LADY . . . ALSO A POEM . . . CALLED THE UNIVERSAL PASSION (1734). *Verse*

A BEAUTIFUL YOUNG NYMPH GOING TO BED (1734). *Verse*
—also contains 'Strephon and Chloe' and 'Cassinus and Peter'.

A PROPOSAL FOR GIVING BADGES TO THE BEGGARS . . . OF DUBLIN; Dublin (1737). *Sociology*

AN IMITATION OF THE SIXTH SATIRE OF THE SECOND BOOK OF HORACE (1738). *Verse*
—written in 1714 and completed by Pope.

THE BEASTS' CONFESSION TO THE PRIEST; Dublin (1738). *Verse*

A COMPLETE COLLECTION OF GENTEEL AND INGENIOUS CONVERSATION (1738). *Social Satire*
—published under the pseudonym of Simon Wagstaff.

VERSES ON THE DEATH OF DR SWIFT. WRITTEN BY HIMSELF (1739). *Verse*
—incorporates part of *The Life and Genuine Character* (1733). The text of the 4 folio editions of 1739, published by Bathurst in London, is inferior to the text of the 6 octavo editions published in Dublin by Faulkner in the same year.

SOME FREE THOUGHTS UPON THE PRESENT STATE OF AFFAIRS; Dublin (1741). *Politics*

THREE SERMONS (1744). *Theology*
—a fourth sermon was added to the second edition of the same year.

DIRECTIONS TO SERVANTS; Dublin (1745). *Social Satire*

BROTHERLY LOVE: A Sermon; Dublin (1754). *Theology*

THE HISTORY OF THE FOUR LAST YEARS OF THE QUEEN (1758). *History*

POLITE CONVERSATION, with introduction, notes and extensive commentary by Eric Partridge (1963).

STELLA'S BIRTH-DAYS: POEMS, ed. Sybil Le Brocquy; Dublin (1967).

Biography and Criticism:

MEMOIRS [OF LAETITIA PILKINGTON], 3 vols (1748-54)
—lively but somewhat fanciful first-hand reminiscences.

REMARKS ON THE LIFE AND WRITINGS OF JONATHAN SWIFT, by John, Earl of Orrery (1752)
—see also P. Delany's more important *Observations on Lord Orrery's Remarks*, 1754.

LIFE OF DR SWIFT, by J. Hawkesworth; Dublin (1755)
—first printed in Vol. I of Hawkesworth's edition of Swift's *Works*.

AN ESSAY UPON THE LIFE, WRITINGS AND CHARACTER OF DR JONATHAN SWIFT, by D. Swift (1735)
—by Swift's cousin, Deane Swift.

LIFE, by W. H. Dilworth (1758).

LIFE, by S. Johnson [in *Lives of the Poets*, Vol. III] (1781).

LIFE, by T. Sheridan (1784).

ESSAY ON THE EARLIER PART OF THE LIFE OF SWIFT, by J. Barrett (1808).

MEMOIRS OF JONATHAN SWIFT, by Sir W. Scott, 2 vols; Paris (1826)
—first printed in Vol. I of Scott's edition of *Works*, 1814.

THE CLOSING YEARS OF DEAN SWIFT'S LIFE, by Sir W. Wilde (1849).

THE ENGLISH HUMOURISTS OF THE 18TH CENTURY, by W. M. Thackeray (1851)
—contains a famous essay on Swift.

JONATHAN SWIFT: Sa vie et ses œuvres, by L. Prévost-Paradol; Paris (1856).

LIFE, by J. Forster (1875)
—only Vol. I was published. The Forster Collection in the Library of the Victoria and Albert Museum, London, contains important manuscript and printed material by and relating to Swift.

SWIFT, by L. Stephen (1882)
—in the 'English Men of Letters' series.

LIFE, by H. Craik (1882: 2 vols, 1894).

JONATHAN SWIFT: A Biographical and Critical Study, by J. C. Collins (1893).

DEAN SWIFT AND HIS WRITINGS, by G. P. Moriarty (1893).

SWIFT IN IRELAND, by R. A. King (1895).

THE ORRERY PAPERS, 2 vols (1903).

SWIFT, by C. Whibley (1917)
—the Leslie Stephen lecture, 1917.

'The Political Significance of *Gulliver's Travels*', by C. H. Firth, *Proceedings of the British Academy*, 1919–1920.

GULLIVER'S TRAVELS: A Critical Study, by W. A. Eddy; Princeton (1923).

SWIFT EN FRANCE, by S. Goulding; Paris (1924).

SWIFT: Les années de jeunesse et 'Le Conte du Tonneau', by E. Pons; Strasbourg (1925)
—the first instalment of a massive but uncompleted critical biography.

SWIFT'S VERSE, by F. E. Ball (1928).

THE SKULL OF SWIFT, by S. Leslie (1928).

DO WHAT YOU WILL, by A. Huxley (1929)
—contains an essay on Swift.

SWIFT, by C. Van Doren (1931).

DEAN SWIFT'S LIBRARY, by H. Williams (1932)
—contains a facsimile of the catalogue of Swift's Library.

THE LIFE AND FRIENDSHIPS OF DEAN SWIFT, by S. Gwynn (1933)
—a popular biography.

JONATHAN SWIFT: A Critical Essay, by W. D. Taylor (1933).

THE WORDS UPON THE WINDOW PANE: A Play in one act, by W. B. Yeats; Dublin (1934)
—a play about a séance in which the spirit of Swift appears. The Introduction has many comments on Swift whom Yeats read with deep interest in the 1920s and 1930s.

THE SCRIPT OF JONATHAN SWIFT AND OTHER ESSAYS, by S. Leslie; Philadelphia (1935).

53

LA PENSÉE RELIGIEUSE DE SWIFT ET SES ANTINOMIES, by C. Looten; Lille (1935).

THE MIND AND ART OF JONATHAN SWIFT, by R. Quintana (1936)
—an important critical study. Revised edition, 1953.

SWIFT'S MARRIAGE TO STELLA, by M. B. Gold; Cambridge, Mass. (1937)
—a careful analysis of all the available evidence relating to this vexed problem.

JONATHAN SWIFT, by B. Newman (1937).

FROM ANNE TO VICTORIA, edited by B. Dobrée (1937)
—valuable essay on Swift by J. Hayward.

JONATHAN SWIFT, DEAN AND PASTOR, by R. W. Jackson (1939).

STELLA, by H. Davis; New York (1942).

SWIFT AND HIS CIRCLE, by R. W. Jackson; Dublin (1945).

JONATHAN SWIFT: A List of critical studies published from 1895 to 1945, by L. A. Landa and J. E. Tobin; New York (1945).

FOUR ESSAYS ON 'GULLIVER'S TRAVELS', by A. E. Case; Princeton (1945)
—defends the 1726 text against Faulkner's revised text of 1735.

THE CONJURED SPIRIT: SWIFT: A Study in the relationship of Swift, Stella and Vanessa, by E. Hardy (1949).

THE SATIRE OF JONATHAN SWIFT, by H. Davis; New York (1947).

SHOOTING AN ELEPHANT, by G. Orwell (1950).
—includes an essay, 'Politics vs Literature', on Gulliver.

SWIFT'S SATIRE ON LEARNING IN 'A TALE OF A TUB', by M. K. Starkman; Princeton (1952).

THE SIN OF WIT: Jonathan Swift as a Poet, by Maurice Johnson; Syracuse (1950).

THE ANGLO-IRISH: Three Representative Types: Cork, Ormonde, Swift, 1602–1745, by B. Fitzgerald (1952).

THE COMMON PURSUIT, by F. R. Leavis (1952)
—contains an important study, entitled 'Swift's Irony'.

THE TEXT OF 'GULLIVER'S TRAVELS', by H. Williams (1953)
—the Sanders Lectures, 1953. A defence of Faulkner's text of 1735.

JONATHAN SWIFT AND THE ANATOMY OF SATIRE: A Study of Satirical Technique, by J. M. Bullitt; Harvard (1953).

SWIFT'S RHETORICAL ART: A Study in Structure and Meaning, by M. Price; New Haven (1953).

JONATHAN SWIFT: A Critical Biography, by J. Middleton Murry (1954).

THE MASKS OF JONATHAN SWIFT, by W. M. Ewald jr. (1954)
—a study of the *personae* adopted by Swift.

SWIFT AND THE CHURCH OF IRELAND, by L. A. Landa (1954)
—an important piece of research.

SWIFT: An Introduction, by R. Quintana; Oxford (1955)
—paperback edition, 1962. A masterly condensation.

SWIFT AND CARROLL, by P. Greenacre; New York (1955)
—a psychological study according to Freudian principles.
THE PEN AND THE SWORD, by M. M. Foot (1957).
THE PERSONALITY OF JONATHAN SWIFT, by I. Ehrenpreis (1958).
IN SEARCH OF SWIFT, by D. Johnston; Dublin (1959).
JONATHAN SWIFT AND THE AGE OF COMPROMISE, by K. Williams (1959).
THEME AND STRUCTURE IN SWIFT'S 'TALE OF A TUB', by R. Paulson; New
    Haven (1960).
DEAN SWIFT, by D. F. R. Wilson; Dublin [1960].
SWIFT'S CLASSICAL RHETORIC, by C. A. Beaumont; Athens, Georgia
    (1961).
THE CURSE OF PARTY: Swift's relations with Addison and Steele, by
    B. A. Goldgar; Lincoln, Nebraska (1961).
SWIFT AND ANGLICAN RATIONALISM: The Religious background of
    'A Tale of a Tub', by P. Harth; Chicago (1961).
JONATHAN SWIFT AND IRELAND, by O. W. Ferguson; Urbana (1962).
SAMUEL BECKETT ET JONATHAN SWIFT: Vers une étude comparée,
    by J. Fletcher; Toulouse (1962).
CADENUS: A Reassessment . . . of the relationship between Swift,
    Stella and Vanessa, by S. le Brocquy; Dublin (1962).
JONATHAN SWIFT: De Englese Voltaire, by J. L. Snethlage; The Hague
    (1962).
JONATHAN SWIFT, by N. S. Subramanyam; Allahabad (1962).
SWIFT: The Man, his Works and the Age, by I. Ehrenpreis (1962–   )
—Vol. I: *Mr Swift and his Contemporaries.* Vol. II: *Dr Swift.*
REASON AND IMAGINATION, ed. J. A. Mazzeo (1962)
—contains an essay by R. S. Crane on Book IV of *Gulliver's Travels.*
DISCUSSIONS OF JONATHAN SWIFT, ed. J. Traugott; Boston (1962).
'GULLIVER'S TRAVELS': A Critical Study, by W. A. Eddy; New York
    (1963)
SWIFT AND THE SATIRIST'S ART, by E. W. Rosenheim (1963).
JONATHAN SWIFT, by H. Davis; New York (1964)
—contains essays on Swift's satire and other studies.
JONATHAN SWIFT: Essays on his satire and other studies, by H. J. Davis
    (1964).
JONATHAN SWIFT: A short character, by N. Dennis (New York 1964,
    London, 1965).
SWIFT, LE VÉRITABLE GULLIVER, by P. Frédérix; Paris (1964).
SWIFT: A Collection of critical essays, by E. Tuveson; Englewood
    Cliffs, N. J. (1964).
SWIFT AND THE TWENTIETH CENTURY, by M. Voigt; Detroit (1964).
SWIFT'S USE OF THE BIBLE: A Documentation and study in allusion, by
    C. A. Beaumont; Athens, Georgia (1965).
SWIFT REVISITED, ed. D. Donoghue; Cork (1965).

TO16836

THE USES OF IRONY: Papers on Defoe and Swift, by M. E. Novak;
Los Angeles (1966)
—includes 'Swift's Use of Irony' by H. T. Davis.

JONATHAN SWIFT: Romantic and cynic moralist, by J. G. Gilbert
(1966).

JONATHAN SWIFT, 1667–1967: A Dublin tercentenary tribute, ed.
R. J. MacHugh and P. W. Edwards; Dublin (1967).

SWIFT, by P. Wolff-Windegg; Stuttgart (1967).

A QUANTITATIVE APPROACH TO THE STYLE OF JONATHAN SWIFT, by
L. T. Milic; The Hague (1967).

JONATHAN SWIFT AS A TORY PAMPHLETEER, by R. I. Cook (1967).

JONATHAN SWIFT AND CONTEMPORARY CORK, by G. Y. Goldberg; Cork
(1967).

FAIR LIBERTY WAS ALL HIS CRY: A Tercentenary Tribute to Jonathan
Swift, ed. A. Norman Jeffares (1967).

SWIFT: Modern Judgements, ed. A. Norman Jeffares (1968).

THE WORLD OF JONATHAN SWIFT: Essays for the tercentenary, collected
and edited by B. Vickers; Oxford (1968).

JONATHAN SWIFT, by K. Williams (1968).

SWIFT'S MOST VALUABLE FRIEND, by S. Le Brocquy; Dublin (1968).

JONATHAN SWIFT: A critical introduction, by D. Donoghue (1969).

SWIFT, by W. A. Speck (1969).

SWIFT: The critical heritage, ed. K. Williams (1970).

JONATHAN SWIFT: A critical anthology, ed. D. Donoghue; Harmonds-
worth (1971).

SWIFT, ed. C. J. Rawson (1971).

JONATHAN SWIFT: An introductory essay, by D. Ward (1973).

GULLIVER AND THE GENTLE READER: Studies in Swift and our time, ed.
C. J. Rawson (1973).

SWIFT: 'GULLIVER'S TRAVELS': A casebook, ed. Richard Gravil (1974).

JONATHAN SWIFT: Major prophet, by A. L. Rowse (1975)
—a lively biography, particularly good about Swift's relationships with
Stella and Vanessa.

WRITERS AND THEIR WORK

SAMUEL JOHNSON: S. C. Roberts
POPE: Ian Jack
RICHARDSON: R. F. Brissenden
SHERIDAN: W. A. Darlington
CHRISTOPHER SMART: G. Grigson
SMOLLETT: Laurence Brander
STEELE, ADDISON: A. R. Humphreys
STERNE: D. W. Jefferson
SWIFT: J. Middleton Murry (1970)
SWIFT: A. Norman Jeffares (1976)
SIR JOHN VANBRUGH: Bernard Harris
HORACE WALPOLE: Hugh Honour

Nineteenth Century:
MATTHEW ARNOLD: Kenneth Allott
JANE AUSTEN:
                    S. Townsend Warner (1970)
JANE AUSTEN: B. C. Southam (1975)
BAGEHOT: N. St John-Stevas
THE BRONTË SISTERS:
                    Phyllis Bentley (1971)
THE BRONTËS: I & II: Winifred Gérin
BROWNING: John Bryson
E. B. BROWNING: Alethea Hayter
SAMUEL BUTLER: G. D. H. Cole
BYRON: I, II & III: Bernard Blackstone
CARLYLE: David Gascoyne
LEWIS CARROLL: Derek Hudson
COLERIDGE: Kathleen Raine
CREEVEY & GREVILLE: J. Richardson
DE QUINCEY: Hugh Sykes Davies
DICKENS: K. J. Fielding
    EARLY NOVELS: T. Blount
    LATER NOVELS: B. Hardy
DISRAELI: Paul Bloomfield
GEORGE ELIOT: Lettice Cooper
FERRIER & GALT: W. M. Parker
FITZGERALD: Joanna Richardson
ELIZABETH GASKELL: Miriam Allott
GISSING: A. C. Ward
THOMAS HARDY: R. A. Scott-James
                    and C. Day Lewis
HAZLITT: J. B. Priestley
HOOD: Laurence Brander
G. M. HOPKINS: Geoffrey Grigson
T. H. HUXLEY: William Irvine
KEATS: Edmund Blunden
LAMB: Edmund Blunden

LANDOR: G. Rostrevor Hamilton
EDWARD LEAR: Joanna Richardson
MACAULAY: G. R. Potter
MEREDITH: Phyllis Bartlett
JOHN STUART MILL: M. Cranston
WILLIAM MORRIS: P. Henderson
NEWMAN: J. M. Cameron
PATER: Ian Fletcher
PEACOCK: J. I. M. Stewart
ROSSETTI: Oswald Doughty
CHRISTINA ROSSETTI: G. Battiscombe
RUSKIN: Peter Quennell
SIR WALTER SCOTT: Ian Jack
SHELLEY: G. M. Matthews
SOUTHEY: Geoffrey Carnall
LESLIE STEPHEN: Phyllis Grosskurth
R. L. STEVENSON: G. B. Stern
SWINBURNE: Ian Fletcher
TENNYSON: B. C. Southam
THACKERAY: Laurence Brander
FRANCIS THOMPSON: P. Butter
TROLLOPE: Hugh Sykes Davies
OSCAR WILDE: James Laver
WORDSWORTH: Helen Darbishire

Twentieth Century:
CHINUA ACHEBE: A. Ravenscroft
JOHN ARDEN: Glenda Leeming
W. H. AUDEN: Richard Hoggart
SAMUEL BECKETT: J-J. Mayoux
HILAIRE BELLOC: Renée Haynes
ARNOLD BENNETT:
                    Frank Swinnerton (1968)
ARNOLD BENNETT:
                    Kenneth Young (1975)
JOHN BETJEMAN: John Press
EDMUND BLUNDEN: Alec M. Hardie
EDWARD BOND: Simon Trussler
ROBERT BRIDGES: J. Sparrow
ANTHONY BURGESS: Carol M. Dix
ROY CAMPBELL: David Wright
JOYCE CARY: Walter Allen
G. K. CHESTERTON: C. Hollis
WINSTON CHURCHILL: John Connell
R. G. COLLINGWOOD: E. W. F. Tomlin
I. COMPTON-BURNETT:
                    R. Glynn Grylls
JOSEPH CONRAD: Oliver Warner

The Novel Today 1967–1975

This edition of *The Novel Today* is the latest in a series of British Council pamphlets on the novel which began with Henry Reed's *The Novel Since 1939* (1945) and continued with studies by P. H. Newby, Walter Allen, Anthony Burgess and Michael Ratcliffe covering the period 1950–67.

The author, Ronald Hayman, makes a personal choice of the fifty-two novelists he finds most impressive among those writing in English in Britain and the Commonwealth today, ranging from well-established writers to some whose first novels belong to the period 1967–75.

The survey is reinforced by a checklist of about a thousand novels by authors working within the period under review which will be of special use to librarians as well as to general readers. The booklet includes portraits of eleven authors.

Ronald Hayman is well known as the author of ten books about contemporary playwrights and for his study of Tolstoy (1970). He was formerly fiction reviewer for the *Sunday Telegraph* (1968–70) and contributes regularly to *The Times* and *The New Review* and to radio commentaries on literature and the arts.

210 x 148mm 96pp. portraits, paperback

LONGMAN FOR THE BRITISH COUNCIL

Poetry Today 1960–1973

Anthony Thwaite's *Poetry Today* is the latest in a series of British Council surveys which began with Stephen Spender's *Poetry Since 1939* (published in 1946), and continued with *Poetry 1945–50* by Alan Ross, Geoffrey Moore's *Poetry Today 1950–57* and Elizabeth Jenning's *Poetry Today 1957–60*. Reviewing the period 1960–73 Mr Thwaite draws particular attention to the dramatic widening of the popular taste for poetry. This phenomenon was first signalled by the Royal Albert Hall mass poetry-reading in 1965 and by the appearance in paperback of cheap editions in thousands of copies – in some cases, tens of thousands – as compared with an average of hundreds in previous years. He examines why more and more people are attracted to poetry and traces the influences of political or humanitarian protest, of pop and of the so-called underground or alternative culture. Elsewhere he reviews the contemporary poetry of Ireland, Scotland and Wales, and discusses developments in various experimental fields, such as concrete poetry, and the influence of the tape recorder in providing a new medium for composition. At the same time, he reminds readers of the enduring influence of poets whose reputation had already been established and who continued to produce new work during the period under survey, and discusses many new poets who have kept to the main tradition.

Anthony Thwaite, who has published four books of poems and a selection in the Penguin Modern Press series, is co-editor of *Encounter* and was formerly literary editor of the *Listener* (1962–65) and of the *New Statesman* (1968–72). He has taught English literature at Tokyo University and the University of Libya, and is a part-time lecturer at the University of East Anglia.

Poetry Today 1960–73 includes a select bibliography, an index and sixteen portraits.

210 x 148mm 104pp. illus. paperback

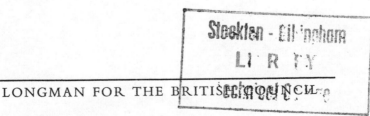
LONGMAN FOR THE BRITISH COUNCIL